Effects of Soldiers' Deployment on Children's Academic Performance and Behavioral Health

Amy Richardson, Anita Chandra, Laurie T. Martin,

Claude Messan Setodji, Bryan W. Hallmark,

Nancy F. Campbell, Stacy Ann Hawkins, Patrick Grady

Prepared for the United States Army

ARROYO CENTER

The research described in this report was sponsored by the United States Army under Contract No. W74V8H-06-C-0001.

Library of Congress Cataloging-in-Publication Data

Effects of soldiers' deployment on children's academic performance and behavioral health / Amy Richardson ... [et al.].
    p. cm.
 Includes bibliographical references.
 ISBN 978-0-8330-5181-3 (pbk. : alk. paper)
 1. Children of military personnel—Education—United States. 2. Children of military personnel—United States—Psychology. 3. Parent and child—United States. 4. Behavior disorders in children—United States. 5. Academic achievement—United States—Psychological aspects. I. Richardson, Amy Frances, 1967-

  LC5081.E34 2011
  379.1'21—dc22

                                     2011006534

The RAND Corporation is a nonprofit institution that helps improve policy and decisionmaking through research and analysis. RAND's publications do not necessarily reflect the opinions of its research clients and sponsors.

Published 2011 by the RAND Corporation
1776 Main Street, P.O. Box 2138, Santa Monica, CA 90407-2138
1200 South Hayes Street, Arlington, VA 22202-5050
4570 Fifth Avenue, Suite 600, Pittsburgh, PA 15213-2665
RAND URL: http://www.rand.org/
To order RAND documents or to obtain additional information, contact
Distribution Services: Telephone: (310) 451-7002;
Fax: (310) 451-6915; Email: order@rand.org

Preface

The increase in the number of soldiers deployed and the number who have deployed multiple times as a result of the Global War on Terrorism has stressed Army families. The environment of persistent conflict, the deployment cycle, and the possibility of a profound lifestyle change brought about by severe injury or even death affects the entire breadth of the Army family. Army Child, Youth, and School Services (CYSS) officials asked RAND to examine the effects of deployment on children's school performance and behavior and recommend changes to ensure that the needs of the children of deployed soldiers are being met.

This report describes the association between parental deployment and student achievement scores among children in North Carolina and Washington between 2002 and 2008. It also presents findings from extensive interviews conducted by RAND Arroyo Center and RAND Health researchers with teachers, counselors, and administrators from elementary, middle, and high schools regarding how deployments of Active Duty, Reserve, and National Guard soldiers have affected children's academic and related behavioral health outcomes. The research team also interviewed civilian and Army experts and stakeholders on child behavioral health. This report offers a set of recommendations to better support these children.

This research was sponsored by the Office of the Assistant Secretary of the Army for Manpower and Reserve Affairs, and was conducted within RAND Arroyo Center's Manpower and Training Program. RAND Arroyo Center, part of the RAND Corporation, is a federally funded research and development center sponsored by the

U.S. Army. Questions and comments regarding this research are welcome and should be directed to the leader of the research team, Amy Richardson, amyr@rand.org.

The Project Unique Identification Codes (PUICs) for the project that produced this document are DAPEM08784 and DAPEM08818.

For more information on RAND Arroyo Center, contact the Director of Operations, Marcy Agmon (telephone 310-393-0411, extension 6419; fax 310-451-6952; email Marcy_Agmon@rand.org), or visit Arroyo's website at http://www.rand.org/ard/.

Contents

Figures

Tables

Summary

Long and frequent deployments, with short dwell times in between, have placed stresses on Army children and families already challenged by frequent moves and parental absences. These stresses may present in the form of social, emotional, or behavioral problems among children at home and at school. With a better understanding of the issues that children face when a parent or guardian deploys, services for military families and children can be more effectively targeted to address those needs.

RAND Arroyo Center was asked by the Army to conduct an analysis of the effects of soldiers' frequent and extended deployments on their children's academic performance as well as their emotional and behavioral outcomes in the school setting. This research included the following objectives:

- To assess academic effects and behavioral health challenges associated with parental deployment;
- To examine programs to support children's academic and school-related behavior during parental deployment and identify the gaps that currently exist;
- To examine the current systems of behavioral health support for these children; and
- Where indicated, make recommendations to support programs to ensure that children's academic and emotional needs are met.

There are three interrelated research components to this study. For all research elements, we examine school-age children of soldiers in the Active force, Army Reserve, and Army National Guard, of all ranks.

1. **Statistical analyses of the correlation between parental deployment and student achievement test scores.** Our research analyzes empirical evidence of the association between parental deployment and dependent achievement test scores for public school students in North Carolina and Washington between 2002 and 2008.

2. **Interviews with school staff about the challenges these students face and suggestions for improvements in support.** We conducted in-person focus groups and interviews with school administrators, teachers, counselors, and other staff involved with children of deployed soldiers to understand the challenges faced by children experiencing parental deployment and by the schools serving these children. We also asked them to identify programs and services that are particularly beneficial or effective in promoting positive outcomes for these children, as well as gaps or areas for improvement that the Army may wish to address to better support children of deployed parents.

3. **Interviews with experts and key stakeholders about the barriers to psychological and behavioral health services for children of deployed soldiers.** We interviewed TRICARE leaders, clinical and pediatric behavioral health specialists, and other key stakeholders including Military Family Life Consultants (MFLCs) on the behavioral health challenges faced by children with deployed parents and their families; programs and services available to support these children; characteristics of these programs or services that are working effectively and might be improved; and gaps in support for these children.

There are a few important caveats to keep in mind. The analyses presented in Chapter Two are based on an examination of achievement test scores. There are many dimensions to academic success and learning not captured in this measure. Also, these tests are administered once a year and so are not sensitive to fluctuations in achievement throughout the course of the year. We were also not able to track children over long periods of time to understand whether the relationship we found between parental deployment and student achievement persists. The findings presented in Chapters Three and Four are based on the perspectives of the teachers, counselors, and school staff who agreed to speak with us; however, we obtained a diverse mix of staff by grade and role to help minimize selection bias. We have not sought to validate these perceptions through more objective measures, nor are we able to determine the extent to which challenges and barriers in services that they identify as stemming from parental deployment may also be ascribed to challenges in the civilian health care sector, schools more broadly, or children with behavioral health needs more broadly. These interviews were also conducted at two large installations and with staff working with Reserve and Guard children across the country. While general findings converged across locations, other communities may experience different challenges. Also, these interviews were conducted in 2008; perspectives and availability of services may have changed since then. We have tried to make note of these changes in services where relevant. We do not believe that any of these limitations affect the nature of the conclusions or the relevance of the recommendations.

Evidence of Academic Challenges That Children Face When Parents Deploy

We present evidence of the association between parental deployment and reading and math achievement for more than 44,000 students in North Carolina and Washington.

Children in North Carolina and Washington whose parents have deployed 19 months or more since 2001 have modestly lower (and statistically different) achievement scores compared to those who have experienced less or no parental deployment. This finding held across states and academic subjects. Grade school students in North Carolina whose parents have deployed 19 cumulative months or more have slightly lower achievement scores than those whose parents have deployed less or not at all. In Washington these differences are more pronounced.

Among the children in our sample, the number of deployments is not associated with academic performance once we account for cumulative months of deployment. Stakeholders and researchers, as well as the media, often express concern over the number of deployments a soldier has seen. While the number of deployments and total months of deployment are clearly related, they are not the same. Having a parent who has deployed 19 months or more continues to be associated with lower test scores, but the number of deployments is not significant.

While longer parental cumulative deployments are associated with lower achievement scores among elementary and middle school students in North Carolina and Washington, this relationship is not statistically significant among high school students. When we examine variation by grade, we find that, in both states, cumulative deployment of 19 months or more is negatively related to achievement scores for elementary and middle school students, but not for high school students.

Otherwise, among the children in our sample, there are no consistent, statistically significant differences in academic performance by length of deployment, rank or component of the soldier, seniority of the soldier, gender of the deploying parent, or gender of the child. Further, the magnitude of the relationship between parental deployment and academic outcomes has not changed over time.

That we see differences in academic performance for children whose parents have deployed 19 or more cumulative months suggests that, rather than developing resiliency, children appear to struggle more with more cumulative months of deployment. These families may benefit from targeted support to help with the special circumstances that more months of cumulative deployment introduce. Elementary and middle school children may also be particularly vulnerable and warrant additional support if these results are confirmed in other studies.

Challenges That Children Face When Parents Deploy

Academic Challenges

Teachers and counselors we interviewed reported that while some children and families cope well with deployment, other families struggle with a range of deployment-related issues that may affect children's academic success. Teachers and counselors noted that some children of deployed parents struggle with homework completion. School staff shared that school attendance can also suffer during parental leave or if the family moves to be closer to grandparents or other support. School staff also indicated that, for some families, their children's academic performance does not seem to be a high priority, particularly in the context of deployments and related stressors. Staff believed parental deployments may also shift the family dynamic at home, which can have a negative effect on academic performance. According to the teachers and counselors we interviewed, students can also have new stress in their lives from additional household responsibilities to fill the void of the deployed parent, or the resident parent may be struggling with mental or emotional problems related to their partner's deployment. Those we interviewed also reported that academic outcomes may be affected if a child's behavioral health is compromised during multiple and extended deployments.

School staff we interviewed had little consistent information on which students are military, when students may be experiencing deployment, and how many students with military parents will be enrolling or leaving the school at any given time. School staff we interviewed, even those close to an installation, reported the need for better information on which of their students are military, and when they are experiencing deployment. Teachers and counselors told us that often the only way they find out is when a child's grades are dropping, and the parent or guardian informs the school that the mom or dad was deployed a month ago. Educators serving Reserve and National Guard families stated that they have an added difficulty in identifying students with a deployed parent, as children of Reserve Component soldiers tend to be a small minority in their schools.

Many of the school staff members we interviewed had little to no connection with military installations. For them, communication with existing Army programs was limited, including contact with the School Liaison Officer (SLO). They shared that when school staff had tried to reach the SLO or other military resources, they were often unable to obtain assistance for their students, or felt that the SLO office required too much information from them before they were willing to help. Educators working with children of Reserve Component soldiers believed they have an even weaker connection with the military. As Reserve Component families are often geographically dispersed, schools serving them may be located far from a military installation, and staff members at these schools may be unprepared to support children whose parents are deployed. Teachers and school staff members also expressed frustration that they did not have a mechanism to involve the Army as a last resort in the rare cases when the child's home life was significantly compromised. Some recalled that before the war, they were able to contact the commanding officer or Army Community Services (ACS), with positive results for the child.

Some of the challenges that teachers and counselors discussed are ones that stem from the high mobility of this population, which can be amplified during deployment. Students lose course credits when they transfer from one school district to another, a challenge voiced across school levels and locations. Students may spend time preparing for state tests or requirements, which can reduce the time spent meeting other core educational objectives. According to those we interviewed, accessing special education services for recently transferred children can also be a tremendous challenge. States vary in their criteria and processes needed to qualify for special education. As a result, with each move to a new state, students may need to be reevaluated for special education services.

Psychological and Behavioral Health Challenges

School staff believed that some parents appear to be struggling more than their children with deployments, which appeared to underlie many of the challenges that these children faced during these multiple and extended deployments. School staff also reported that although deployments are becoming a normal part of children's lives, for many children, resiliency appears to be waning. Those we interviewed reported that in the first years of the war, there was more anxiety in classrooms about what was occurring, but now the response in the classroom is increasingly one of apathy. School staff also believed that schools are becoming the stable place or sanctuary for students when home life is chaotic or uncertain. Finally, school staff members felt they often did not have adequate assistance in helping students and parents access psychological and behavioral health services, and school leaders requested that more effort be placed on providing assistance for ways to obtain these services.

MFLCs may provide necessary student, family, and staff support in schools, but those we interviewed felt monitoring and evaluation of this program could be improved. The MFLC program is broadly designed to provide support and assistance to Active, National Guard and Reserve soldiers, military family members, and civilian personnel. MFLCs provide training information and support to school staff and nonmedical consultation to students and families. Although MFLCs are housed in schools, they are not considered school staff, and records are not kept on the students or their progress. While these policies help reduce fear of stigma from seeking behavioral health services, they also limit the ability to assess the benefits of the program and areas for improvement.

The stakeholders we interviewed felt the number of available providers with training in child and adolescent services is low. Ensuring that families have timely access to psychological and behavioral health services for children can be challenging, particularly when there is a national shortage of psychological and behavioral health providers. Further, the number of providers who have specific training in child and adolescent development is much smaller. According to stakeholders, in addition to the absolute shortage, there is wide geographic variation in provider availability. Stakeholders believed that limited acceptance of TRICARE among many civilian providers further reduced access, particularly for activated National Guard or Reserve families or families enrolled in TRICARE Reserve Select, who may be less connected to military health providers.

Stakeholders perceived that some providers do not have good grounding in military culture. While many of the providers who see TRICARE patients have current or prior military experience, newer providers to this community may not have as much understanding of the unique needs of military families. Behavioral health providers who primarily serve civilian populations may be relatively new to the issues and concerns of military families.

According to the school staff and stakeholders we interviewed, availability and coverage of certain behavioral health services, as well as prevention, screening, and early intervention, are not adequate and vary geographically. One critical area raised almost universally was the availability of residential treatment facilities. In addition, despite advances in creating individualized treatment plans, those we interviewed believed many of the services remain fragmented, making it difficult for children facing multiple needs to have a coordinated care plan. Other services that may not be sufficiently covered or available include in-home services and treatment for eating disorders. Interviewees also argued for more attention to behavioral health issues in schools and primary care settings to address the needs of the child before the issue becomes more severe and requires the services of child and adolescent psychiatrists specifically.

According to most providers, engagement of families in behavioral health services can be challenging. Those we interviewed found that parents may not perceive the child's need for services, stigma may deter them from seeking services for their children, and logistical challenges can reduce engagement in services over time.

Recommendations

Our analysis leads to several possible ways in which the Army can address the challenges faced by military children before, during, and after parental deployment. Most of these changes come with a financial cost, and in some cases these costs are likely to be considerable. Estimating the costs of each of these possibilities, however, is outside the scope of our analysis. Therefore, we offer these as recommendations for the Army to *consider*, as our analysis suggests that there could be benefits from implementing them. Before the Army pursues any of these changes, we recommend a careful analysis of the costs, both fiscal and nonfiscal, associated with them. In addition, it is important to note that the research on which many recommendations are based was conducted in 2008 and 2009. We have made an effort to note some of the most relevant actions taken by the Army since then.

Recommendations to Address Academic and School-Based Needs

1. Address student academic challenges. Providing additional military resources to support students with their schoolwork, particularly during parental deployment or before and after extended absences from school due to parental leave, may help students who are struggling academically. For the rare cases when a child is struggling with deployment and the school is unable to engage the parent, we recommend that the Army develop a set of procedures for schools to seek ACS support to engage the unresponsive parents. We also recommend that the Army consider increasing transportation services for youth, particularly to facilitate their participation in after-school activities. Transportation can be a challenge for military children, who may therefore be unable to participate in after-school activities. While state and local dollars often fund support for those populations, installations may be able to offer additional transportation support. This support might include adding a bus stop that allows children to be dropped off closer to home or adding an extra run at the end of the day. Installations in some locations have also purchased buses and created new routes, which is likely a more expensive alternative but does not require obtaining city support.[1]

2. Address academic challenges related to high mobility. While children of military parents have traditionally been highly mobile due to parental change of assignment or location, parental deployments have compounded this problem. A further challenge is that

---

[1]   Since 2008, when these interviews were conducted, the Army contracted with Tutor.com to provide online academic tutoring for Army-connected youth, and added 199 buses to provide transportation to and from youth programs.

during block leave, children may have extended periods of mobility and absence from school. The Army should continue to advocate for full adoption and prompt, effective implementation of the Interstate Compact on Educational Opportunity for Military Children, which addresses state variation in the transfer of records, course sequencing, graduation requirements, and other issues.

3. Improve the flow of information to schools. Many of the concerns raised by school staff members point to the critical need to improve the flow of information to schools. Information flow may be improved by expanding efforts to educate school staff about the military, developing methods to inform schools about which children are military and the timing of parental deployments, providing school counselors a way to easily and effectively access information on military support and services available to families, striving for a more collaborative relationship between SLOs and schools, and revitalizing the "Adopt-A-School" program.[2]

Recommendations to Address Behavioral Health Needs

1. Continue to build behavioral health capacity by increasing the number of providers who are trained in child and adolescent behavioral health issues. Behavioral health service capacity could benefit from continued tuition support for students pursuing advanced degrees in behavioral health fields as well as from developing other support programs.

2. Expand provider understanding of military culture. Developing provider training on military culture and potential impacts of deployment, including the types of emotional issues children may experience, could also improve understanding of the specific needs of these children. Providers should also include pediatricians, school nurses, and behavioral health specialists.

3. Continue to expand models for improving access for hard-to-reach populations. Expanding models for improving access for hard-

---

[2] Since 2008, the Army has introduced military culture courses to educate faculty and school staff on the unique needs of military-connected youth, and added an additional 41 SLOs, for a total of 141 Garrison SLOs.

to-reach or remote youth populations, including telepsychiatry, might also improve access to services. Discussions with military behavioral health providers suggested that telepsychiatry was increasingly being used for those youth who were far from a military hospital or unable to access local behavioral health services. Telepsychiatry programs have been found effective in reducing childhood depression and show promise as a feasible and effective tool more broadly.

Reserve Component families are typically dispersed, making it difficult to connect with other Reserve and National Guard families. Promoting social networks among these families could foster relationships among these children, minimize their feelings of isolation, and strengthen the general sense of community. Social networks might be promoted by organizing frequent and regular regional or statewide social events and developing a social networking website specifically for youth of Reserve and National Guard soldiers.

4. **Consider strategies for improving the availability of prevention, screening, and early identification, particularly in schools and other community settings.** These strategies may include augmenting school behavioral health services for youth and families of deployed soldiers, which can help overcome limited access to services and stigma. Enhancing integration of behavioral health services with primary care, particularly in those clinics and hospitals serving military populations, would also help identify issues early on. While the integration of these services has become more common in nonmilitary settings, many of the providers we interviewed felt that the potential of these models had not been fully realized for their clients. In civilian sectors, pediatricians are increasingly identifying and treating psychological and behavioral health disorders, including depression, among their patients as well as exploring alternative technologies to facilitate screening.

5. **Improve family engagement in behavioral health services.** Recruitment and retention of families in child behavioral health services is difficult across populations, but for military families, issues of time, stigma, and other factors may make it challenging to stay in services. There is evidence that certain models of engagement intervention have shown improvements in "show rates" between the first and second patient visits.

6. **Improve assistance to school staff in helping students and parents access services.** Providing school counselors, nurses, and other staff with current information on military and community behavioral health services may assist in improving linkages to timely and appropriate care even though counselors cannot refer students themselves.

7. **Improve evaluation of the MFLC program by integrating some outcomes-based measurement.** Our interviews examined the benefits of structuring a program that was short-term and relied on the MFLC "outside" presence to overcome many of the stigma-related barriers associated with behavioral health services. However, according to the stakeholders we interviewed, the low level of monitoring and evaluation of services makes it exceedingly difficult to assess whether and how the program is having a positive impact on youth and families.

Recommendations for Future Research

1. **Monitor the academic performance of children with parents who have deployed for long cumulative periods of time to understand the association between deployment and academic performance over time.** To understand whether the association between cumulative parental deployment and academic performance of children persists, and whether it extends beyond these children, the Army should examine longitudinally the academic performance of children of soldiers. Our analysis included children from 2002 to 2008, and could only track students as long as they remained in that state. Studying the long-term relationship of parental deployment and academic performance, even as children move across states, would help the Army understand whether these associations persist.

2. **Quantitatively assess effects of deployment associated with other academic performance measures.** Given our qualitative findings noting that, at least for some children, there are academic challenges associated with parental deployment, it will be important to extend future analyses beyond annual test scores. There is a need to conduct analyses on additional metrics of academic success and school behavior that may be more sensitive to the rapid changes that deployment brings. Such analyses may also help to identify early indicators that could signal potential struggles with parental deployment. Such met-

rics should include academic engagement (e.g., attending to tasks in class, coming prepared to class), quarterly grade point average, school connectedness, disciplinary issues, extracurricular involvement, on-time high school or grade level completion, and postsecondary activities including college and/or military service entrance.

3. Examine whether deployment is having an impact on symptoms or behavioral health diagnoses. It is not clear whether any observed increase in symptomatology among children of Army soldiers translates into higher rates of diagnosable psychological and behavioral health disorders. The distinction between symptomatology and diagnoses is an important one, as the programmatic and policy solutions to address each scenario vary significantly.

4. Examine trends in met and unmet behavioral health needs using claims data. An important and, as of yet, untapped resource for understanding the effect of parental deployment would be an analysis of claims data that links behavioral health service utilization with characteristics of parental deployment. To date, there is relatively little analysis of behavioral health service use and whether services are available to address needs. While such an analysis would shed light on the impact of parental deployment on children's behavioral health issues, it would not capture unmet needs—those individuals who need services but are not seeing a provider. This is a critical issue, since in the general population 75 to 80 percent of children and youth in need of psychological and behavioral health services do not receive them. However, there is little empirical evidence quantifying the scope and extent of the problem among military children. In addition, further investigation is warranted into whether children are receiving recommended treatment protocols by appropriate personnel. No studies to date have examined whether children are seeing clinicians trained at a level that is appropriate for their current needs.

5. Identify a comparable civilian cohort to assess similarities and differences in behavioral health service use rates. Given the hypothesis that parental deployment is related to an increase in behavioral health problems, it is reasonable to want to directly compare rates of disorders between military and civilian children and adolescents. This comparison, however, is challenging because there is no centralized database of health care claims and diagnoses in the civilian population. In addition, while epidemiologic research provides population-level estimates in the community, the estimates vary widely depending on the diagnostic method used, age of the study sample, and time frame. The criteria used to diagnose a child or adolescent with a behavioral health disorder may also vary widely among military providers, since the majority of reporting providers are social workers, psychologists, and pediatricians rather than child psychiatrists, who may use more standardized assessment tools. Direct comparisons between rates of behavioral health disorders among military and civilian populations will require a study that could assess similar claims data, with a comparable population, during the same time period. Data do not currently exist to facilitate such a direct comparison.

6. Examine the alignment of current Army and civilian programs with youth academic and behavioral health needs. Based on this and other studies on youth from military families, there has been a stronger call for evaluation of the current programs that serve this population. It also will be important to examine whether and to what extent the actual content of existing Army and civilian programs is aligned with the academic and behavioral needs identified in our analysis. This study was not intended as a comprehensive program gap analysis whereby we inventory the landscape of programs serving Army youth and assess the match of these services to needs, including target subgroups by location, component, age, or gender. However, a study that explores this content consistency is needed to highlight where curriculum and training fit the types of needs reported by school staff, including youth stress, parent engagement, and academic progress.

Acknowledgments

We are deeply grateful to all the individuals who gave us their time and valuable input for this research. Foremost we thank Susan Johnson, Assistant Deputy for Child, Youth and School Services, Office of the Assistant Secretary of the Army for Manpower and Reserve Affairs, and P.K. Tomlinson, Chief, Soldier Support Programs Branch, Soldier and Family Readiness Division, Office of the Assistant Chief of Staff for Installation Management, for their considerable time and support given throughout the course of this research.

We also wish to thank Carmen Marino and C. Van Chaney of Army Child, Youth and School Services (CYSS) for sharing with us their knowledge of Army support services and for reviewing early recommendations. This report also benefited from the insight provided by M.A. Lucas and Helen Roadarmel of CYSS; COL Elspeth Cameron Ritchie and COL Ricky Malone of the Office of the Army Surgeon General; and COL James Polo, Office of the Assistant Secretary of the Army for Manpower and Reserve Affairs, Health Affairs.

Analysis of achievement scores would not have been possible without the considerable support provided by Kara Bonneau and Claire Mushkin of the North Carolina Education Data Research Center and by Lisa Ireland and Kristina Quimby of the State of Washington Office of the Superintendent of Public Instruction. We are also grateful for the willing participation and valuable insight of the school administrators, teachers, counselors, and behavioral health service providers and stakeholders we interviewed; we thank them for their thoughtfulness and openness.

Within RAND, we thank Bruce Orvis, Terri Tanielian, Michael Hansen, and Jerry Sollinger for their support, insight, and valuable comments during the course of this research effort. Finally, Dr. Lou Mariano, Senior Statistician, RAND, and Dr. Marleen Wong, Assistant Dean and Clinical Professor of Field Education, University of Southern California, provided detailed and constructive suggestions which greatly improved this document.

Glossary

ACS	Army Community Services
AOR	Area of Responsibility
ARNG	Army National Guard
CTS	Contingency Tracking System
CYSS	Child, Youth and School Services
DEERS	Defense Enrollment Eligibility Reporting System
DMDC	Defense Manpower Data Center
DoD	Department of Defense
DoDEA	Department of Defense Education Activity
E1	Private
E2	Private
E3	Private First Class
E4	Specialist/Corporal
E5	Sergeant
E6	Staff Sergeant
E7	Sergeant First Class
E8	Master Sergeant/First Sergeant
E9	Sergeant Major/Command Sergeant Major/Sergeant Major of the Army
FRG	Family Readiness Group
HQDA	Headquarters, Department of the Army
IOM	Institute of Medicine

JBLM	Joint Base Lewis-McChord
MCEC	Military Child Education Coalition
MFLC	Military Family Life Consultant
MHAT	Mental Health Advisory Team
NGS	New Generation System
O1	Second Lieutenant
O2	First Lieutenant
O3	Captain
O4	Major
O5	Lieutenant Colonel
O6	Colonel
O7	Brigadier General
O8	Major General
O9	Lieutenant General
O10	General
OEF	Operation Enduring Freedom
OIF	Operation Iraqi Freedom
OMK	Operation Military Kids
PTSD	Post-Traumatic Stress Disorder
RESPECT-Mil	Re-Engineering Systems of Primary Care Treatment in the Military
SLO	School Liaison Officer
STAR	Student/Teacher Achievement Ratio
USAR	U.S. Army Reserve
WASL	Washington Assessment of Student Learning

CHAPTER ONE

Introduction

Multiple deployments and the accompanying increased pace of military life have placed stresses on Army children and families already challenged by frequent moves and parental absences. To sustain the forces needed, the Army has had to rely heavily on the U.S. Army Reserves (USAR) and Army National Guard (ARNG), who comprise roughly one-third of soldiers deployed (Bonds, 2010). Typically, soldiers will deploy for twelve months,[1] although this can vary, as Special Forces and medical personnel often deploy for shorter periods; there are also reports of longer deployments (Cox, 2009). While stated Army policy is to allow two years dwell time between deployments for Active Component soldiers and four years for Reserve Component soldiers, average dwell times since 2001 among soldiers with multiple deployments have been well below these goals for Active, Reserve, and National Guard components (IOM, 2010, p. 28).[2]

Deploying soldiers often leave behind families; slightly more than half of soldiers are married, and 40 percent have children (Department of Defense, 2007). The increased operational tempo, environment of persistent conflict, and possibility of a profound lifestyle change brought about by severe injury or death affects the entire breadth of

---

[1] From early 2007 to August 2008, deployments were on a fifteen-month schedule.

[2] For this research, Reserve and National Guard soldiers who have been activated are considered part of the Reserve and National Guard forces to distinguish them from Regular Army soldiers who serve full-time. Active Duty Component soldiers who serve full-time are referred to as Active to avoid confusion with activated Reservists, who are considered by the Army as "on Active Duty."

the Army Family. The stresses of parental deployment may present in the form of social, emotional, or behavioral problems for all military youth at home and at school.

With a better understanding of the issues that children face when a parent or guardian deploys, services for military families and children can be targeted more effectively to address those needs. Analysis of the perspectives of front line responders, such as teachers and school counselors, is also important to examine more closely the effect of parental deployment on the emotional and behavioral outcomes of children and youth in the school setting.

1.1. What We Know About the Impact of Deployment on Children and Families

A number of studies have examined the specific effects of deployments since September 11, 2001 on children in various age ranges. Adolescent children of deployed soldiers experience higher rates of emotional difficulties, and child difficulties increased with the total number of months deployed (Chandra et al., 2010). A survey of Army spouses of deployed soldiers found that among children between the ages of five and twelve, one-third could be at high risk for psychological and social problems, particularly among parents who reported high levels of parenting stress (Flake et al., 2009). Chartrand and colleagues (2008) examined even younger children, aged three to five, and found that those with a parent deployed had more behavior problems than those without a deployed parent. Child maltreatment and neglect also increase during parent deployment, particularly when the nondeployed parent is a civilian woman (Gibbs et al., 2007).

Some studies have also explored differential responses of children to deployment. Findings have been mixed; there is evidence that younger children experience larger negative behavioral effects, but others have found the older children also experience negative effects (Jensen, Martin, and Watanabe, 1996; Chandra et al., 2010). Girls appear to experience greater difficulties with reintegration (Chandra et al., 2010). Also, families with younger parents, and parents with less education were all more likely to have children with psychological and behavioral health problems during parent deployment (Flake et al., 2009). Response to deployment may also vary based on the rank and component of the soldier. Spouses of Reserve officers report coping better with deployment than do spouses of Reserve enlisted soldiers (Casteneda et al., 2008). Previous research also suggests that Active and Reserve Component soldiers' families may have different experiences during deployment. For example, spouses of Reserve Component soldiers reported poorer emotional well-being compared to spouses of Active-Duty soldiers (Chandra et al., 2011).

There is more limited evidence on the effects of parental deployment on the academic performance of children. While a few studies suggest that children experiencing parental deployment have slightly lower academic performance compared to children who are not experiencing parental deployment, these studies utilize academic performance data of children of Active-Duty soldiers collected prior to 2001 or among children attending Department of Defense (DoD)-sponsored schools and may not provide an accurate assessment of the impact of the current deployment cycle on the academic performance of most children (Pisano, 1992; Lyle, 2006; Engel, Gallagher, and Lyle, 2010). Since 2001, for example, soldiers and other service members have experienced multiple redeployments, often with little time in between, deployment of high numbers of women and of parents of young children, and a high number of military personnel who survive severe injuries that in previous wars would have resulted in death. It is not known whether these differences impact academic achievement of children experiencing parental deployment.

Further, we know very little about the possible differential impact of deployments on children from families in the Reserve and Guard components. The size of the available pool of Active personnel and the extended nature of the conflicts have required an unprecedented use of the Reserve and National Guard, who have been activated to serve far longer deployments than most had ever expected or experienced. These children may have less familiarity with the Army and deployment, particularly if their parents did not serve in the Regular Army, and fewer resources to help them cope with the stress that accompanies it. Relatedly, we do not know how the children who attend public schools are responding to post-2001 deployments, despite the fact that two-thirds of Army dependents attend public schools.

To our knowledge, no studies have examined the effects on academic achievement of post-2001 parental deployments among public school children, among children of Reserve and Guard soldiers, or among children of both officers and enlisted soldiers. We are also aware of no studies of school-aged children from military families that have included the perspectives of school staff.[3] These are important gaps to fill, as early success in school is predictive of subsequent educational attainment, employment with higher earnings, and better health outcomes (Ensminger and Slusarcick, 1992; Leventhal, Graber, Brooks-Gunn, 2001).

1.2. Study Purpose and Methodology

RAND was asked by the Army to conduct an analysis of the effects of soldiers' frequent and extended deployments on their children's academic performance as well as their emotional and behavioral outcomes in the school setting. This includes the following objectives:

- To assess academic effects and behavioral health challenges associated with deployment;
- To examine programs to support children's academic and school-related behavior during parental deployment and identify the gaps that currently exist;
- To examine the current systems of behavioral health support for these children; and
- Where indicated, make recommendations to support programs to ensure children's academic and emotional needs are met.

There are three distinct but interrelated research components to this study. One component included statistical analyses of the relationship between parental deployment and achievement test scores of

---

[3] Chartrand et al. (2008) focused on child care providers and their experience with children younger than school-aged.

children; these findings are presented in Chapter Two. We also conducted interviews with administrators, teachers, and counselors about
the challenges these students face and their suggestions for improvements in support, as well as interviews with experts and key stakeholders about the barriers in behavioral health services for children of
deployed soldiers. The findings of these two research components are
presented together in Chapters Three and Four.[4] For all research elements, we examine school-age children of soldiers in the Active force,
USAR, and ARNG based in the United States.

1.2.1. Analysis of Academic Testing Scores

Study Population. Our study population includes dependents
of soldiers in all Army components. Nearly two-thirds of children of
Active Component soldiers attend public schools, and among children
of Reserve and Guard soldiers, the percentage is likely higher because
DoD schools are not an option (20 percent of Active-Duty children
attend DoD schools).[5] We examine the children of enlisted soldiers and
commissioned officers.

We analyze students from North Carolina and Washington for
several reasons. Both states are home to large Army installations that
have seen multiple deployments. Fort Bragg, North Carolina, is the
largest Army installation by population, with 52,280 Active-Duty soldiers, 12,624 Reserve Component soldiers, and 62,962 Active-Duty
family members. Joint Base Lewis-McChord (JBLM) (formerly known
as Fort Lewis), Washington, is also large, with 27,000 soldiers and
52,486 family members.[6] Both states also have significant Reserve and
Guard populations. Finally, North Carolina and Washington main-

---

[4] Throughout this report, psychological, emotional, and mental health are included in the
term "behavioral health."

[5] Data derived from DMDC Status of Forces Survey of Active Duty Spouses, 2006. For
more detail, see Table B.1.

[6] Military Homefront, U.S. Department of Defense, "Military Installations: Ft. Lewis."
As of March 1, 2010:
http://apps.mhf.dod.mil/pls/psgprod/f?p=MI:CONTENT:3139022256467421::::P4_
INST_ID,P4_CONTENT_TITLE,P4_CONTENT_EKMT_ID,P4_CONTENT_
DIRECTORY:5050,Installation%20Overview,30.90.30.30.30.0.0.0.0,1

tained academic records in a centralized database for the time period of interest, making it possible for us to analyze student records across the states.

Data Sources. To examine the relationship between parental deployment and academic performance, we linked data by student from two sources: (1) state education data on achievement testing scores and student demographics, and (2) DoD and Army data on soldiers and deployment.

Academic data were then linked to soldier-parent data, which included deployment data as well as personnel data such as rank, component, and years of service. Our analysis includes all dependents of soldiers who listed North Carolina or Washington as their permanent or temporary residence at some point during the period 2000–2007 in the Defense Enrollment Eligibility Reporting System (DEERS) and attended public school. DEERS maintains personnel and benefits information for Active, retired, and Reserve uniformed service personnel, eligible family members of Active, retired, and Reserve uniformed service personnel, as well as DoD civil service personnel and some DoD contractors. Deployment data, obtained from the Contingency Tracking System of the Defense Manpower Data Center (DMDC), is captured as a monthly bivariate data element, which is equal to 1 if the soldier is deployed that month and 0 otherwise.[7]

Measuring Academic Achievement. Achievement test data were available from 2002, soon after the start of Operation Enduring Freedom (October 7, 2001), through 2007 (for North Carolina) and 2008 (for Washington).[8]

---

[7]   The Contingency Tracking System (CTS) Deployment File includes all U.S. military personnel who have been deployed in support of contingency operations in Iraq and Afghanistan from September 11, 2001 to the present. It is updated monthly and includes a separate individual record for every deployment event, for each member. For the Army, deployment begins when a soldier is on the ground in an Area of Responsibility (AOR) and is therefore eligible for hostile fire pay. A soldier is entitled to a month of hostile fire pay if he or she spent any portion of that month in theater.

[8]   Research on North Carolina was conducted in FY2007–2008, and research on Washington was conducted in FY2008–2009.

In North Carolina during the period under examination (2002–2007), elementary and middle school students took End-of-Grade (EOG) Reading and Math Tests each year, which are administered to most students in June. These tests measure the goals and objectives as specified in the 2004 North Carolina English Language Arts Standard Course of Study and Mathematics Standard Course of Study. At the high school level, all students are also required to take an End-of-Course (EOC) Test in English I and Algebra I (although advanced students may take these courses and exams before high school) to "sample a student's knowledge of subject-related concepts as specified in the North Carolina Standard Course of Study and to provide a global estimate of the student's mastery of the material in a particular content area" (North Carolina End-of-Course Tests). Because grade school and high school students in North Carolina take tests that measure different competencies, these results are modeled separately. To allow for comparisons across grades, subjects, and years, original scaled test score results were normalized relative to the statewide distribution in each grade and subject with a mean of 0 and a standard deviation of 1.

In Washington, students were administered the Washington Assessment of Student Learning (WASL), which consists of examinations over four subjects (reading, mathematics, science, and writing), to measure their ability to meet the state's academic standards. The WASL is given to students from grades 3 through 9, though it is not required in the ninth grade. In each year during the 2002–2007 time frame, reading and math were administered; science and writing were administered only in select grades. Scaled test score results for Washington were also normalized relative to the statewide distribution in each grade and subject.

It should be noted that during our period of investigation, No Child Left Behind modified the consequences of performance on state assessments in ways that caused many schools and districts to approach their assessments differently. Many states in response reevaluated their assessment content; North Carolina, for example, rescaled various tests at different points in time during the analysis period. Using normalized scores allows for a common interpretation relative to one's peers, regardless of content changes, although the scores throughout the time period may not be exchangeable.

It may also be useful to understand the relative performance of North Carolina and Washington in education. The standardized tests that form the basis for this analysis are specific to the state, but the National Assessment of Education Progress (NAEP) survey includes a nationally representative sample and assesses reading and math, as well as other subjects. On NAEP assessments in 2003, 2005, and 2007, for grades 4 and 7, North Carolina performed above the national average in all math tests but below in four of the six reading tests, and Washington performed above the national average in all tests.

Analyses. Multivariate, cross-sectional regression analyses were conducted, by state and by subject, controlling for soldier component, rank, years of service, seniority, race, education level, age, and gender, and student age, gender, socioeconomic status (as indicated by eligibility for free or reduced lunch), grade, and year. Analyses accounted for clustering by child (in North Carolina) and school (in Washington). Additional methodological details may be found in Appendix A.[9]

1.2.2. Interviews with Administrators, Teachers, and Counselors

We conducted in-person focus groups and interviews with school principals and other administrators, as well as with teachers, counselors, and other staff involved with children of deployed soldiers to understand the challenges faced by children with deployed parents and their families. Counselors included a range of staff from academic counselors to school social workers and psychologists. We also sought to

---

[9] Often in education analyses, researchers will perform a statistical adjustment to account for schoolwide variables, such as the quality of the teaching and classroom size, that may influence a student's academic testing score. However, this was not possible with the North Carolina sample, as many students changed schools during the period of analysis (2002–2007). When trying to estimate the effects, we no longer had a nested structure, and the effect on each student's test score can be attributable to multiple schools. Therefore, the results we present here are cluster-adjusted by student (because a student may appear in our sample multiple times), but not by school. There were some models that could be fit even after cluster-adjusting for school (for example, when we evaluated the results by year or by grade). The results were consistent with those found when cluster-adjusting by student, so we do not believe that this alternative adjustment affected our conclusions.

identify issues that schools face while supporting these children, to identify what programs and services are particularly effective in promoting positive outcomes for children, as well as what gaps or areas for improvement the Army may wish to address to better support children of deployed parents.

We conducted the focus groups and semi-structured interviews at twelve schools in the spring of 2008. The twelve schools comprised one elementary school, one middle/junior high school, and one high school in each of four districts. Two of the districts served the majority of families at one Army installation, and the other two served the majority of families at another installation in a different region of the country.[10]

These installations were selected due to their continued and high rates of deployment. The selection of location for the interviews was made independently of the selection of states for the quantitative analysis. Because family socioeconomic status (SES) can make a difference in school outcomes, we compared median household income and family poverty rates from the U.S. Census (2000) for the communities surrounding the selected locations to the rates in communities surrounding other large Army installations. When the rates of the communities around the Army installations are arrayed, the rates for those communities at the installations where we conducted interviews fell in the middle third, with one exception on one measure. Further specificity would undermine the confidentiality of the sites. Assuming stability in the rates from 2000 to the interviews, the comparison suggests that the children living in the communities around the installations were not at particularly high risk or low risk for problems associated with SES compared to other large Army installations. While the quantitative analysis includes all school-aged children of soldiers in the state, the interviews were conducted with school staff on or near Army installations. Interviewing staff at schools with a relatively high density of military children helped ensure that teachers and counselors were familiar with the challenges faced by children when their parents deploy. Therefore, while the quantitative and qual-

---

[10] To preserve confidentiality of those with whom we spoke, we do not identify the states in which the qualitative interviews were conducted.

itative components of the research inform one another, their results are not directly comparable. In addition, because our interviews were conducted in areas that have seen significant deployment, school staff may have observed more challenges among children of deployed soldiers than would be observed in areas where there have been fewer deployments.

The two closest school districts to the post were selected for involvement in the study and individual schools were identified by district-level staff or superintendents as having the highest proportion of military youth. At each school, approximately two administrative staff, three counselors, and six teachers participated in the study (N = 132 staff, in total). When possible, interviews and focus groups were held separately for administrators, counselors, and teachers. In addition, we conducted 16 phone interviews across the country with teachers, counselors, and administrative staff serving Army Reserve or National Guard children, who may be more isolated and live further from a military installation. Staff were identified through snowball sampling—wherein those we interviewed recommended others whom we might interview in areas with high concentrations of Army Reserve and National Guard soldiers, regardless of location—and also through organizations that serve schools with Reserve and National Guard children.

The findings we present do not reflect an exhaustive accounting of every issue raised by school staff, but rather highlight some of the major concerns and recommendations that emerged related to the academic and associated behavioral health needs of these children, particularly during deployment. Further, given the unique experiences of Reserve and Guard families, we highlight issues that are especially salient for these students.

There are a few caveats to these findings that are important to keep in mind. First, this research is based on the perspectives of those teachers, counselors, and school administrators who agreed to speak with us, and so the sample is neither random nor representative. Second, our findings are based on interviews from school staff at two large installations and from staff working with Reserve and Guard children across the country. While general findings converged across locations, other communities or schools may experience different challenges. Third, most of these interviews were conducted between March and June 2008, and changes in perspective may have occurred since then. There have also been changes in the availability of services, many of which we have noted throughout this report. We do not believe, however, that any of these limitations to the research affect the nature of the conclusions or the relevance of the recommendations.

1.2.3. Interviews with Behavioral Health Experts and Key Stakeholders

Semi-structured telephone interviews were designed to elicit expert views on the behavioral health challenges faced by children with deployed parents and their families; programs and services available to support these children; characteristics of these programs or services that are working effectively and that might be improved; and gaps in support for these children. Interviews with behavioral health care experts also included a discussion of the system of care available to dependents of Army soldiers in the Active and Reserve components. In total, the project team conducted 12 individual and group interviews with TRI-CARE leaders, clinical and pediatric behavioral health specialists,[11] and other key stakeholders, including Military Family Life Consultants (MFLCs), who provide behavioral health support in schools.

While our mandate was not to create a comprehensive accounting of all behavioral health services available to Army families, we sought to identify and highlight some of the primary sources of care available to these families across the medical and nonmedical sectors. Likewise, a systematic assessment of ongoing Army activities in each of the domains highlighted in this report was beyond the scope of this project; however, we do acknowledge and refer to activities that we learned about in the process of conducting the interviews and writing the report.

---

[11] Most of the specialists we interviewed worked off post, and 60 percent were uniformed while 40 percent were civilian.

1.3. About This Report

This report provides a synthesis of the study findings. Chapter Two presents evidence of the relationship between deployment and academic performance among children in the states of North Carolina and Washington. Chapter Three discusses the academic challenges for these children while their parents prepare for deployment, deploy, and then return from deployment. Chapter Four examines the behavioral health challenges for those children and the gaps in care to meet their needs. Chapter Five provides recommendations for addressing the challenges and gaps in programs and services.

CHAPTER TWO

Evidence of Academic Challenges That Children Face When Parents Deploy

This chapter presents evidence of the relationship between parental deployment and reading and math achievement of students in North Carolina and Washington. We compare the scores of children whose parents have deployed with the Army in support of Operation Enduring Freedom (OEF) in Afghanistan and Operation Iraqi Freedom (OIF) in Iraq to Army children who have not experienced parental deployment.

2.1. Description of the Sample

Our analysis includes all school-age children of Army soldiers who resided in North Carolina and Washington between 2002 and 2008, regardless of their proximity to an Army installation. We compare the achievement scores of children whose parents have deployed to those whose parents have not deployed. Our sample includes more than 44,000 children, but because attributes of the child and parent may change over time (the soldier-parent may change components or ranks, for example), we describe the sample in 2007, the most recent year of data from North Carolina. This 2007 sample consisted of 13,966 students in North Carolina and 3,066 students in Washington who were dependents of Army soldiers (Table 2.1). Of these, roughly two-thirds were children of Active soldiers, 14 percent were of USAR soldiers, and 21 percent were of ARNG soldiers, numbers that mirror those

Table 2.1
Sample Descriptive Statistics

	Total Army Population	Deployed Army Population	North Carolina	Washington
N (soldier)	1.1 million	947,664		
N (child)			13,966	3,066
Parent				
Component				
Active Duty (%)	49	61	65	63
Reserve (%)	18	13	14	15
National Guard (%)	33	25	21	22
Officer/enlisted				
Officer (%)	13	14	13	17
Enlisted (%)	85	86	87	83
Child				
Gender, male (%)			51	51
Race/ethnicity				
White (%)	66		53	66
Black (%)	18		37	19
Other (%)	16		10	15

SOURCE: Total Army Data from Department of Defense (2007); deployed Army population data from DMDC as cited in IOM (2010).

for the population of soldiers who have deployed since 2001. Among the soldier-parents of the children in our sample, the proportion of roughly one officer for five to seven enlisted soldiers is also consistent with both the deployed Army population and total Army population. The racial composition of the soldier-parents of children in the Washington sample is the same as for the Army as a whole, while there is a greater proportion of African-American soldier-parents in the North Carolina sample than in the Army as a whole.

Soldier-parents in our samples from both states have faced heavy deployment schedules, even for the Army (Table 2.2). As of 2007, two-thirds (Washington) to three-fourths (North Carolina) of soldier-parents have deployed at least once, and more than one in five soldier-parents in both states were deployed at the time of the academic achievement test in June 2007. Among those who have deployed, 23 percent of soldier-parents in the North Carolina sample and 10 percent

Table 2.2
Sample Parental Deployment Statistics

2007	Total Army	North Carolina*	Washington
N (soldier)	1.1 million		
N (child)		13.966	3,066
Total sample:			
Ever deployed (%)	51	74	67
Deployed in the past year (%)		42	35
Is deployed currently (%)	16	23	22
Among those who have deployed:			
One deployment (%)	63	48	59
Two deployments (%)	37	28	31
Three or more deployments (%)		23	10
Number of deployments since 2001 (mean)		1.9	1.6
Months deployed since 2001 (mean)		13.1	13.0

SOURCES: http://veterans.house.gov/Media/File/110/2-7-08/DoDOct2007-DeploymentReport.htm as of April 20, 2010.

* Deployment data for North Carolina through June 2007; Washington through December 2007; Deployment data for Army from the CTS Deployment File for Operation Enduring Freedom and Iraqi Freedom, as of October 31, 2007.

of those in the Washington sample have deployed three or more times. Deployments have been heavy across components. In North Carolina, 81 percent of Active soldiers have ever deployed and half had deployed in the past year; half of USAR soldiers had ever deployed, and two-thirds of ARNG soldiers had ever deployed.

2.2. The Relationship Between Deployment and Achievement Test Scores

2.2.1. Notes on Interpreting Results

Even though estimates of the effect of deployment were estimated accounting for other covariates, for simplicity we present only the deployment effect estimates in the tables below. More detailed results including standard error estimates for the coefficient estimates presented in this chapter may be found in Appendix D. Models were run separately for each outcome, with results presented collectively in the following charts to facilitate comparison across outcomes (e.g., reading, math). As a reminder, the tests administered to grade school and to high school students in North Carolina measure somewhat different subject areas and therefore their outcome scores must be modeled separately. Students in Washington do take tests in similar subject areas reflecting the curriculum at each respective grade, and we model those together. Statistical significance was assessed at the standard 5 percent significance level and the more stringent 1 percent level.

The parameter estimates presented are standardized effect sizes. All the outcomes studied are standardized, which allows for the effect sizes to be compared to effects observed in other studies. In making these comparisons, however, the reader should keep in mind that these tests may measure somewhat different skills and abilities. Therefore, rough comparisons of magnitude are appropriate, but statistical inferences of differences are not. Researchers in education often cite the Tennessee Student/Teacher Achievement Ratio (STAR) class size reduction study as a source for comparison. Using a controlled scientific experiment, researchers found that reducing class size from between 22 to 26 students to 13 to 17 students had a significant effect on student achievement, with an effect size ranging from 0.15 to 0.25 (Zimmer et al., 2009; Word et al., 1990).[1] A recent analysis of benchmarks found in 61 other random assignment studies and in meta-analyses also found effect sizes that are consistent with this range (Hill et al., 2008).

There is a modest, consistent, negative relationship between cumulative months deployed and academic outcomes across the two states and two subjects examined.

The primary goal of this research is to determine whether parental deployment is undermining the academic performance of the child. We therefore first tested the simple relationship between cumulative months of parental deployment since 2001 and performance

---

[1]   Results of this study were used to justify class reduction efforts in primary grades in 30 states, and Senate proposals for federal assistance for class size reductions were motivated by Project STAR research (Whitmore, 2006, p. 3).

on achievement tests. We found a negative relationship between the cumulative months a parent had deployed and achievement test scores across states (North Carolina and Washington) and subjects (reading and math) where one additional month of deployment is associated with a lower student achievement outcome. The size of this relationship, however, is quite modest; each additional cumulative month of parental deployment is associated with a 0.003 to 0.004 point lower normalized scale achievement score. For the typical 12-month deployment, this translates to a difference of 1/25 to 1/20 of a standard deviation, which is considerably smaller than the effect of class size observed in the Tennessee STAR study (Figure 2.1 and Tables D.1 and D.2). In Washington, for example, where the average WASL reading score is 409 (with a standard deviation of 25), a 0.004 difference in normalized score will be equivalent to a 1.18 point difference in the reading scale score.

Figure 2.1
The Relationship Between Deployment and Achievement Test Scores: Cumulative Months of Deployment Modeled Linearly

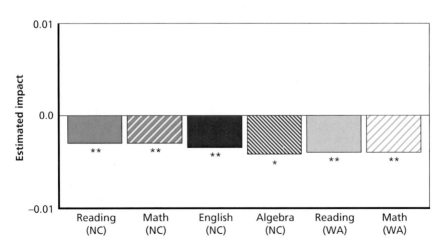

**statistically significant at 1 percent level.
*statistically significant at 5 percent level.

There appears to be a threshold whereby children experiencing cumulative parental deployment of 19 months or more score significantly lower on achievement tests compared to those experiencing less cumulative parental deployment.

While cumulative months deployed modeled linearly (as above) is negatively associated with student achievement test scores, we wanted to test whether there is a point or threshold of length of deployment that is associated with significantly lower academic achievement. The relationship between deployment and academic outcomes may vary during the course of a single deployment (e.g., the first month of deployment may have a stronger association with academic outcomes compared to the fifth or sixth month into a parental deployment when daily routines have been reestablished). This "emotional cycle of deployment" may include multiple shifts from stability to instability and emotional disorganization back to stability again (Morse, 2006).[2]

To examine this, we modeled cumulative months deployed in six-month increments (0, 1–6, 7–12, 13–18, 19–24, and 25 or more months). While few months of cumulative parental deployment show no association with achievement scores, the relationship becomes statistically significant and meaningful for students in both states after 19 months of cumulative deployment. For students in North Carolina, the relationship of cumulative months is somewhat linear. Children in both grade school and high school whose parents have deployed 1–6 cumulative months at the time of the test see no difference in test scores compared to those whose parents have not deployed. Those whose parents have deployed 7–12 months and 13–18 months respectively have lower average test scores compared to those whose parent has not deployed, although the impact is small and significant only at the 5 percent significance level. Longer parental deployments of

---

[2] Studies on the effects of deployment among soldiers have also found nonlinear associations (we are not aware of any studies examining this for outcomes for children). For example, one study found that soldiers with fewer months of cumulative deployment (up to 12 months) were more likely to reenlist than their peers who had not deployed, but those with 12 or more months were less likely to reenlist (Hosek and Martorell, 2009, p. 49).

19–24 months and 25+ months are significantly associated with lower test scores for grade school students (who take reading and math tests) with meaningful effect sizes; the relationship between parental deployment and achievement among high school students (who take English and algebra tests) is not significant, possibly due to the smaller sample size in the group.[3] In Washington, the association between parental deployment and academic outcomes is seen only once parental deployment exceeds 18 months. (Figure 2.2 and Table D.3.) As a result of these findings and to simplify the analysis, we categorize cumulative deployment as 0 months, 1–18 months, and 19 months or more hereafter.

Figure 2.2
The Relationship Between Deployment and Achievement Test Scores: Cumulative Months of Deployment Modeled as Six Categorical Variables

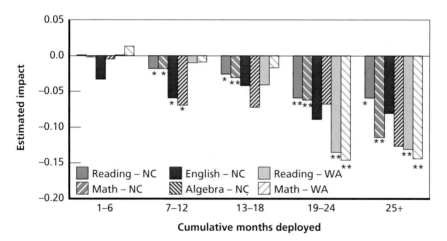

**statistically significant at 1 percent level.
*statistically significant at 5 percent level.
RAND *MG1095-2.2*

---

[3]   As a reminder, sample sizes are as follows: North Carolina high school: English 6,847, algebra 4,762; for North Carolina grades 3 through 8: reading 49,554, math 49,982; Washington grades 4, 7, and 10: reading 12,902, math 12,960.

Children whose parents have deployed 19 months or more since 2001 have modestly lower (and statistically different) achievement scores. This finding held across both states and academic subjects.

Grade school students in North Carolina whose parents have deployed 19 or more cumulative months have reading scores that are lower by 0.05 standard deviations and math scores that are lower by 0.06 standard deviations. In Washington, students whose parents have deployed 19 or more cumulative months have scores that are lower by 0.13 standard deviations in reading and 0.14 standard deviations in math. The results for Washington are on par with the 0.15–0.25 effect size observed with smaller class size in the benchmark Tennessee STAR study and are considered meaningful. The results for North Carolina are more modest, suggesting that cumulative deployments of 19 months or more have an effect size of about one-third the impact that would be seen by sharply reducing class size (Figure 2.3 and Table D.4).

In the two states examined, the number of deployments is not associated with academic performance once we account for cumulative months of deployment.

Stakeholders and researchers, as well as the media, often express concern over the number of deployments a soldier has seen. While the number of deployments and total months of deployment are clearly related, they are not the same.[4] Typical deployments last 12 months, but soldiers in the Special Forces and medical branches, for example, will deploy for much shorter periods of time.

To test the hypothesis that the number of deployments, rather than total months deployed, has a stronger association with academic outcomes, we added the number of parental deployments to the model. Having a parent who has deployed 19 months or more continues to be associated with lower test scores, but the number of deployments was

---

[4]   Among the parents of children in our North Carolina sample, the Pearson correlation coefficient is 0.79.

Figure 2.3
The Relationship Between Deployment and Achievement Test Scores:
Cumulative Months of Deployment

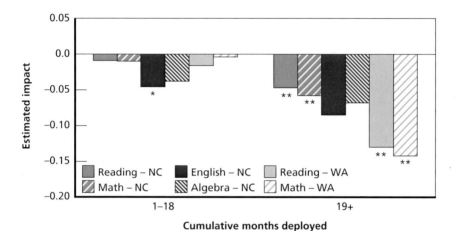

Cumulative months deployed

**statistically significant at 1 percent level.
*statistically significant at 5 percent level.
RAND *MG1095-2.3*

generally not significant. There was, however, one exception. In North Carolina, English scores among high school students were positively correlated with the number of times a parent has deployed. Scores of these students also experience the strongest negative relationship with cumulative parental deployment of 1 to 18 months and 19 months or more, and this effect size is larger than observed when the number of deployments is not included in the model (for North Carolina in English, this relationship is now statistically significant). There is a similar but insignificant pattern among children in Washington. It may be that when the association between cumulative deployments and lower achievement scores is stronger, shorter individual deployments (and hence more deployments) can help mitigate this relationship (Figure 2.4 and Table D.5).

Figure 2.4
The Relationship Between Deployment and Achievement Test Scores:
Cumulative Months of Deployment and Times Deployed

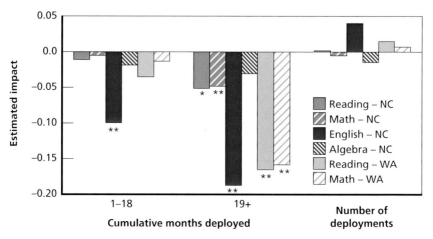

**statistically significant at 1 percent level.
*statistically significant at 5 percent level.
RAND MG1095-2.4

2.3. The Relationship Between Deployment and Achievement Test Scores by Characteristics of the Parent and Child and by Year

We examined whether the nature of the relationship between deployment and achievement scores varies depending on characteristics of the parent or child and whether it has changed over time. Including statistical interactions in our model identifies whether a particular characteristic is associated with even greater vulnerabilities to effects of deployment on achievement scores. For example, while an increase in the number of months of parental deployment may be associated with lower reading scores, this association may be stronger for boys than girls.

2.3.1. Variables Examined in This Analysis

Rank. We examined whether the rank of the soldier affects the impact that deployment has on a child's academic performance. Many enlisted soldiers have a high school diploma or equivalent and perform specific job functions, while most commissioned officers have college degrees or equivalent and perform managerial and leadership functions. While deployed, the two sets of soldiers may also face different, although overlapping, experiences, with the officers, particularly those in the more senior ranks, less exposed to combat. The differences in socioeconomic status and roles performed by the officer-parent may help mitigate the effects of deployment on the child.

Component. The component of the parent may also play a role in the child's response to deployment. Most children of Active soldiers live on or near an Army installation, attend schools with other children of soldiers, have access to resources to support Army families, and have experience with extended absences of their soldier-parent due to training, unaccompanied assignments, and, although on a more limited scale before 2002, deployments.[5] Most children of Reserve and National Guard soldiers, on the other hand, do not live near a military installation, attend schools with few, if any, other children of soldiers, have relatively limited access to Army family support services, and, prior to 2002, had less experience with soldier-parent absences attributable to the Army.

Seniority. We also examined whether the seniority of the soldier-parent played a role in exacerbating or modifying the effect of deployment on student achievement. Junior soldiers are more likely to be exposed to combat and life-threatening circumstances, and their families have had less experience with the Army.

Gender of Soldier-Parent. We tested whether the gender of the soldier-parent was associated with better or worse student achievement outcomes. In general, women continue to be the primary caregivers to

---

[5]   Children of Active Army parents, who typically live on or near an Army post and among other Army families, may also experience more support of the war within their community, which may be beneficial. For example, an adolescent's belief that the American public supports the war may reduce stress during parental deployment (Wong and Gerras, 2010).

their children regardless of their employment status (Coltrane, 2000). In a study of pre-2001 deployment (when female deployment was less common), Lyle (2006) found that children of female soldier-parents who deployed experience greater declines in math test scores than children of deployed male soldier-parents. Because women constitute only a small percentage of the deploying force (14 percent) many other studies on the impact of deployment on children have not had sufficiently large samples to examine this question (IOM, 2010).

Gender of Child. We also examined whether the gender of the child was associated with a differential response to parental deployment. Studies of psychological and behavioral health have found mixed results. One study of post-2001 deployment found that girls reported more challenges during deployment, while a study of deployments before 2001 found the opposite result (Chandra et al., 2010; Jensen, Martin, and Watanabe, 1996). A study of achievement scores among children in Department of Defense Education Activity (DoDEA) schools found that male children struggle more with deployment (Engel, Gallagher, and Lyle, 2010).

Grade of Child. We also compared the association between deployment and academic performance for elementary (grades 3 through 5), middle (grades 6 through 8), and high school students. Younger children may not fully comprehend why a parent must leave, and older children may have trouble coping with parental deployment during a critical and rapid stage of social and emotional development, which is challenging in the most supportive and stable of environments (Huebner and Mancini, 2005). Some research on the effect of deployment on student achievement has found that the negative effect of parental deployment on academic scores is more pronounced on elementary-age children (grades 3–6) than on secondary-age children (grades 7, 8, and 10) (Engel, Gallagher, and Lyle, 2010; Lyle, 2006).

Year. Finally, we examined whether the relationship between parental deployment and academic achievement changed over time since the start of OIF and OEF. It may be that children and families have grown more accustomed with time to anticipate deployments as they have become more frequent since 2001. This would be particularly true for the families of Reserve and Guard soldiers, who had little reason to expect regular deployments before 2001. In addition, as discussed in Chapter One, the Army and DoD, as well as civilian organizations, have added significant resources to support Army families year by year. These factors may have mitigated the effect of deployment on children since 2001. On the other hand, steady deployments have stretched thin even those who have not deployed, and the increased possibility of parental deployment can produce anxiety for a child even in the absence of deployment orders. We compare children in 2005, 2006, and 2007 (for North Carolina) and 2006, 2007, and 2008 (for Washington) to children in earlier years.

2.3.2. Results

While elementary and middle school students in the two states examined see lower achievement scores with more cumulative months of deployment, high school students may not.

When we examine variation by grade, we found that in both states, cumulative deployments of 19 months or more were most strongly associated with lower achievement scores for middle school students. For middle school students in both states and for both subjects, there is a strong and meaningful negative relationship between deployment and achievement scores. In Washington, cumulative deployments of 19 months or more are also associated with lower achievement scores among elementary-aged children, although this is not the case for North Carolina. Among high school students in both states and across both subjects, cumulative deployment of 19 months or more is not associated with score declines. (In North Carolina, cumulative deployments of 1 to 18 months, however, were associated with lower scores in both English and algebra.) It may be that high school students are better able to maintain their routines and are less dependent on their parents for forms of support including after-school transportation, help with homework, and emotional support (Figure 2.5 and Table D.6). As mentioned previously, it also may be that this relationship is not statistically significant due to smaller sample sizes.

Figure 2.5
The Relationship Between Deployment and Achievement Test Scores:
Cumulative Months of Deployment by Grade

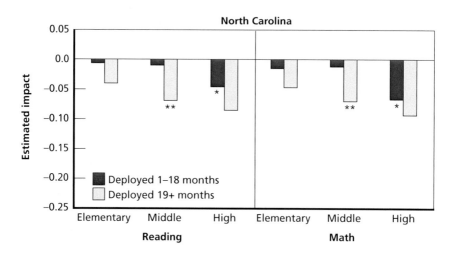

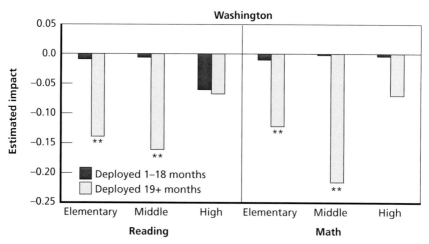

**statistically significant at 1 percent level.
*statistically significant at 5 percent level.

Otherwise, there are no consistent, statistically significant differences by rank or component of the soldier, seniority of the soldier, gender of the deploying parent, or gender of the child, nor has the relationship worsened since 2001.

The association between parental deployment and achievement scores is similar across rank and component; the interactions are small and statistically insignificant. The exception to this may be found in Washington, where the reading scores of children of Reserve/Guard enlisted soldiers who have deployed between 1 and 18 cumulative months and 19 or more are relatively low. This pattern is not replicated, however, in reading scores in North Carolina, nor in math scores in Washington (Table D.7). We also find no difference in academic response to parental deployment among children of soldiers of junior, mid-grade, and senior ranks (Table D.8).

Similarly, we found no evidence that the gender of the deploying parent or the gender of the child is associated with greater academic challenges. The interaction is not significant for either shorter or longer periods of cumulative deployment (Tables D.9 and D.10).

Finally, we found no differences over time; the relationship between parental deployment and student achievement did not change as the conflicts in Afghanistan and Iraq continued. It is possible that both sets of exacerbating and mitigating factors are at work—that the rising pace of operations has stretched troops thin and increased stress on the soldier-parent and anxiety among children, while at the same time families have come to expect and prepare for deployment more than before and that programs have been developed to better support them during deployment—and that these might neutralize one another (Table D.11).

2.4. Summary and Discussion

Our analyses suggest that in North Carolina and Washington, parental deployments are associated with modestly lower achievement test scores. This relationship is strongest for children who have a parent that has deployed 19 months or more since 2002; children of parents with cumulative deployment up to 18 months see little to no impact on achievement test performance. This relationship is stable across a wide variety of dimensions, including the state (North Carolina and Washington), characteristics of the soldier (component, rank, seniority, gender), characteristics of the child (grade, gender, although high school students may fare better than younger children), and across years.

That we see a stronger negative relationship between parental deployment and student achievement for children whose parents have deployed 19 or more cumulative months and little if any relationship at lower levels of deployment suggests that children, rather than developing resiliency, appear to struggle more with more cumulative months of deployment. Longer total time away appears to erode any initial resilience. It may be that the child absorbs additional responsibilities while the parent is away and this may be difficult to sustain. Longer cumulative absences of the parent may also strain family dynamics. These families may benefit from targeted support to help with the special circumstances that longer cumulative deployments introduce. Elementary and middle school children may also be particularly vulnerable and warrant additional support if these results are confirmed in other studies. The following chapters explore the issues that these children are facing in greater depth and offers recommendations for improving this support.

The presence of a negative association between parental deployment and achievement scores independent of a variety of parental and child characteristics suggests the need for a strategy to support children of deployed soldiers that is widespread across components as well as officers and enlisted soldiers. This is consistent with the approach taken thus far, where support is offered irrespective of rank, seniority, or other factors, though individual programs may be targeted to specific families, children, or needs. The Army should work to ensure that similar levels of support are also offered across the Active, Reserve, and National Guard components.

There are a few limitations to this analysis that should be recognized. First, we have examined the relationship between parental deployment and achievement test scores. There are many dimensions to academic success and learning that are not captured in this measure. Second, we could not control for the students' achievement prior to parental deployment as is done in "value added" analyses, which would have eliminated any unknown biases. Third, tests are administered once a year and are not sensitive to fluctuations in achievement throughout the course of the year. Other studies have found that students struggle more just after deployment and reintegration. Fourth, we could not track military children over long periods of time. Active Army soldiers move states frequently, and we could not track them after they moved out of North Carolina or Washington.

Finally, while our results suggest that there is a relationship between cumulative parental deployment and student achievement test scores, it is possible that at least some of this association is attributable to factors not explored in our analysis. The primary concern would be that parental deployment is not exogenous to student academic achievement, but previous research has found that the two variables are exogenous (Engel, Gallagher, and Lyle, 2010). Nonetheless, it is possible that there are factors not accounted for in our analysis that would be associated with both parental deployment and student academic achievement.

CHAPTER THREE

Academic Challenges That Children Face When Parents Deploy

The school staff we interviewed reported that while some children and families cope well with deployment, other families struggle with a range of deployment-related issues that have an impact on children's academic success. For example, a child not only has to adjust to the deployment of their parent, but must also cope with the additional stressors facing their nondeployed parent, including raising children without the day-to-day support of their partner, managing finances, and addressing household responsibilities (Chandra et al., 2010; Castaneda et al., 2008). Based on the perspectives of the school officials we interviewed, these stressors are particularly pronounced for families who are facing repeated or extended deployments. As a result, teachers and counselors reported that some children are being asked to "grow up fast" by helping the nondeployed parents or guardians take care of the house and siblings, and take on responsibilities not typically requested of young children.

This chapter describes the perspectives of teachers, counselors, and school administrators from elementary, middle or junior high, and high schools regarding the impact of deployments on academic outcomes for children experiencing parental deployment. As described earlier, we conducted focus group interviews in person with administrators, teachers, and counselors at schools on or near two Army installations, and by phone with teachers and counselors who had worked with children of USAR and ARNG soldiers. We also interviewed several MFLCs across the country who provide support and assistance to military family members in the school setting, supporting not only the children and families experiencing parental deployment, but also school staff working with these children. Where relevant, we include their observations, and identify them explicitly.

Chapters Three and Four examine the academic and behavioral health challenges that children face when their parents deploy. Our findings in these chapters are intended to inform, not replicate, the findings presented in Chapter Two, that children whose parents have deployed for 19 months or more cumulatively have modestly lower achievement scores. Rather, Chapters Three and Four look more closely at the nature of those challenges that may help explain those lower achievement scores. Chapters Three and Four also examine challenges some children face that may not be not reflected in achievement scores. For example, a child may exhibit signs of distress apparent to a teacher or counselor (such as poor homework completion, lower grades, moody behavior, or disengagement) that might not translate to lower achievement scores. Alternatively, a child may struggle with and then recover from a deployment before a test has been administered, or struggle after the test has been administered. In these cases, a teacher or counselor might observe students challenged by parental deployment even when achievement test score comparisons do not capture this.

In the following sections we summarize the perspectives of school teachers, counselors, and administrators we interviewed on student academic challenges, staff challenges in addressing military student and family needs, and common student issues exacerbated by deployment. To identify themes, we used techniques from the analytic tradition of grounded theory, to read a sample of transcripts and look for examples that suggest processes, actions, assumptions, and consequences. We then created a coding scheme to organize data into relevant domains, and conducted an analysis separately of a sample of notes to ensure that our coding scheme effectively captured all theme areas. We then compared our codes across three researchers to ensure consistency in our coding. Study team members summarize the data first by domain, further analyzing it by relevant themes and ensuring that themes were supported by multiple respondents and not simply one participant.

Because we relied largely on focus groups, it is not possible to quantify the degree to which each issue is or was a widespread problem within the Army. We also did not seek to validate our findings with additional, more-objective data. However, for the purposes of our analysis, we prioritized those themes that were voiced by multiple respondents (i.e., a theme was voiced in more than one focus group, across all school levels [elementary, middle, and high school], and across the two study locations). Findings that were articulated by a single group or person that were particularly insightful for specific populations (e.g., issues specific to elementary-aged children or those whose parents are in the Reserve or Guard) were also included, but are explicitly noted. As such, themes described in Chapters Three and Four were widespread challenges and issues for Army children and youth as articulated by those we interviewed.

Data are presented below by general theme, with themes that were reflected by multiple groups provided first in each theme area. Further detail may be found in Appendix B.

3.1. Student Academic Challenges

3.1.1. According to the Teachers and Counselors We Interviewed, Two Significant Academic Challenges for Some Children of Deployed Parents Are: (1) Homework Completion and (2) School Attendance

Teachers across all focus groups and interviews noted that homework completion is a major hurdle for some children of military parents, particularly during deployment. For a variety of reasons, these teachers observed, some parents and guardians do not have the time or energy to help children with homework. As a result, these children turn in incomplete assignments, if they turn in any assignment at all. Teachers in all groups reported that some parents use the deployment as an excuse, noting, for example, that the child's father is the one who is skilled in math and that he is unavailable to help the child. As an example of this sentiment, one teacher mentioned:

> As a whole the homework issue is really big. They don't do it; they don't have someone sitting over their shoulder to help them. Homework is more challenging when you don't have support at home. *(Teacher, Middle School)*

During deployment, some families will relocate to be closer to their parents' sources of support, often grandparents or close friends. In this case, teachers across the groups and interviews described that children will often disengage from their schoolwork once they learn that they will be moving, even if they are not scheduled to leave for another month (teachers have similar concerns for children who are moving due to a permanent change of station, regardless of parental deployment). Particularly concerning, however, is that some of the families do not end up moving due to a change in orders or personal plans, but by then it is too late to get back on track, according to those we interviewed.

> When kids think they are going to be moving, they stop putting effort into school—so what's the point. They don't understand that an F here will follow them. And some don't end up moving, but they have given up. *(Counselor, High School)*

An issue expressed almost unanimously across school personnel pertains to the academic disruption the child experiences when he or she is taken out of school for extended periods, such as when a parent is home on leave. While schools and school personnel want to support the family during this time, those we interviewed expressed concern about the amount of classroom time the children miss, particularly for the older children, and about the disruption of routine and stability for the younger children. Several teachers across focus groups and interviews reported working out agreements with the parents so that the child could keep up with classwork. Teachers emailed assignments or gave them out in advance, but in many cases the children returned not having completed the work. Missing extended periods of school in the short term puts a child at risk for failing a class, but in the long term, significant learning gaps may occur. Teachers across school levels reported, however, that parents were more inclined to take younger children out of school for extended periods of time, with older children left at home to attend school. One teacher explained:

> We want to support kids in bonding with their families, but by the end of year, they could have missed about a third of the year. No matter how many resources we have, we can't help them if they aren't here. It is almost impossible to make up those [attendance] gaps and this becomes exponential over time. We have seventh graders at fourth grade level. *(Teacher, Middle School)*

3.1.2. The Teachers We Interviewed Reported That for Some Children, Parental Disengagement During Deployment Can Undermine Academic Priorities and Be Challenging for School Staff

Individual and family factors influencing academic resiliency may vary from child to child. School staff members across focus groups and interviews noted that important factors associated with such resilience include the value placed on education by the parent or guardian responsible for the child during the deployment, parental psychological health, and the level of supervision in both the home and the community. As an example, one teacher mentioned:

> If there is a strong foundation from the beginning, then it pretty much stays that way even when the parent is gone. You can take one component out and it still works. *(Counselor, High School)*

Teachers and counselors across groups and interviews shared that if the child and family are in the "normal range" of academic and social functioning, they will experience some difficulties, but if there were issues prior to the deployment, the deployment may magnify these problems.

One challenge is that during deployments, children do not always live with a nonmilitary parent. Rather, teachers reported, the child may reside with a wide-ranging set of guardians including stepparents, grandparents, extended family, neighbors, or friends. In some cases they may move around several times over the course of their parents' deployments, particularly if the child exhibits psychological, emotional, or behavioral problems not easily handled by the guardian. This lack of stability has clear implications, for both academic performance and school attendance, as well as psychological and emotional outcomes of the child. One teacher mentioned:

> The families are really getting extended and there is so much confusion about "who I belong to." If you are trying to figure out who your family is, it is very difficult to focus on what is going on in school. *(Teacher, Elementary School)*

Parental deployments may also shift the family dynamic at home, which can have a negative effect on academic performance, teachers and counselors shared. While some children cope well with deployment and exhibit little change in academic performance, school staff observed that others are struggling. Teachers noted that in many military families, fathers set rules and boundaries, and when this presence is gone, mothers are left with this responsibility. This can create questions about who is in control of the household. School staff across grade level also noted that the problem of parental inattention may extend beyond increased absenteeism or not completing homework.

School staff across groups and interviews also expressed that it can be difficult for them to engage parents as well. Teachers speculated that parental psychological and behavioral health and literacy issues were contributing factors, and they expressed frustration in repeatedly trying to contact parents, or in parents not showing up for parent-teacher conferences or meetings regarding student academic issues.

Teachers and school staff members across groups and interviews also expressed frustration that they did not have a mechanism to communicate with leadership in the deployed parent's unit to intervene in the rare cases when the child's home life was significantly compromised. While school staff members reported that they were reluctant to get families in trouble, many participants across school levels and locations felt that they needed more guidance on how to notify and involve the Army as a last resort, and recalled that before the war they were able to contact the commanding officer or Army Community Services (ACS) with positive results for the child.

> We used to be able to call a commanding officer to indicate that the person needs to show up for IEP [individualized education plan] and the officer would set it up and they would [show up]. Now, I don't know how to make it happen, who to call [when the parents are disengaged]. *(Counselor, Elementary School)*

3.1.3. The Teachers We Interviewed Perceive That Some Students Have New Stress in Their Lives from Additional Household Responsibilities

While some students are finding ways to address the deployment, including avoiding home, the teachers and counselors we interviewed expressed that many students are also called upon to assume more responsibility to fill the void of the deployed parent or if the nonmilitary parent is struggling with psychological or behavioral problems related to their partner's deployment. Many teachers and counselors, particularly those from middle and high schools, voiced concern about the amount of responsibility placed on children during a deployment.

For example, teachers noted that older siblings may be asked to take on more responsibility including taking care of younger siblings or becoming a co-parent.

> They can't do their homework because they are too busy doing their chores. I had a little girl a couple of years ago that had to get her siblings up in the morning, give them breakfast, dress her brothers and sisters, get their backpacks on, and get them ready for school before she could get ready to go to school, and then she would have to walk [them to school] and she said, "I am just so tired." *(Teacher, Middle School)*

3.2. Barriers to Addressing Child Academic Needs

3.2.1. Administrators Reported That Schools Have Little Consistent Information on Which Students Are Military, When Students May Be Experiencing Deployment, and How Many Students with Military Parents Will Be Enrolling or Leaving the School at Any Given Time

School staff across all school locations, even those geographically proximal to an installation, reported the need for better information on which of their students are military, and when they are experiencing deployment. Teachers and counselors across grade levels explained that often the only way they find out is when a child's grades are dropping, and the parent or guardian informs the school that their mom or dad was deployed a month ago.

> Ones that I do know about came through the back door. It wasn't "My husband is being deployed." Usually comes in through 504s,[1] academic challenges, that is where I find out about them. *(Counselor, Middle School)*

Educators we interviewed serving USAR and ARNG families believed that they and their colleagues have an added difficulty in identifying students with a deployed parent, as children of Reserve Component soldiers tend to be a small minority in their schools. These educators perceived that school staff members for these USAR and ARNG families are less aware of the possibility that a student may be connected to the military, let alone that a parent may be deployed.

> Unless the parent identifies that they are in the Reserve or they are in the Guard and they are going to be deployed, the teachers don't know. I think the biggest gap is a better way to identify kids whose parents are in the Reserves. The knowledge that these kids exist and what kinds of services they can benefit from—that could help us immensely. *(Administrator)*

---

[1] Refers to Section 504 of the Rehabilitation Act, which specifies that no one with a disability can be excluded from participating in federally funded programs or activities, including elementary, secondary, or postsecondary schooling.

I was doing an Emotional Disturbance evaluation, and the kid saw my [Support the Troops] bracelet, and he told me his dad, brother, and uncle were all deployed. If he hadn't said something, I wouldn't have known—I wouldn't have thought to ask. *(Counselor, Middle School)*

For all school levels and locations, staff felt that having a better sense of who is affected will help them serve their students better and provide support for the student and family before the child's academics suffer.

In addition to not knowing which children are affected, schools serving a high proportion of military students also reported staffing challenges, as they do not know how many children are expected to arrive or leave their school over the coming months. As a result, these schools shared concerns about being understaffed and others reported being overstaffed, believing that accurate and current information from the military could avoid those problems.

We have no solid information about who is coming and when. No "Here is a list of kids coming," "Here is who will be impacted." We don't know what the stable numbers are at school, so we don't know how many staff are needed for the fall. *(Counselor, Middle School)*

3.2.2. Many School Staff Members We Interviewed Had Little to No Connection with Military Installations

Another commonly reported concern across locations and school levels was that school staff members have little or no connection with the military installation. Communication with existing Army programs is limited, including contact with the School Liaison Officer (SLO). SLOs function as liaisons between schools and the Army, originally to help ease the transition between schools when a family relocates, but more recently also to help families and schools with deployment-related issues. SLOs also provide information and assistance to families and school officials as necessary, and work collaboratively with schools to improve education for military children.

While a small number of schools reported having good connections with their SLO, a more common sentiment was that the schools "haven't heard from them [the SLO] in years." Some of these schools had stopped pursuing SLO services out of frustration over having received no response or delayed responses as well as over the amount of information needed from the school about the child. When the connection was successful, however, those we interviewed found the services to be useful.

> We have a school liaison, but when we call, they're slow to respond. I had to give them a lot of information, but I didn't have it all. I didn't understand why I had to find out all of the information when the liaison was on base, and has access to everything. We would really like better coordination to make the lines smoother. *(Counselor, Middle School)*

> We want to advocate for families, but don't know where to start and we haven't had a point of contact in years. *(Counselor, Elementary School)*

> No information trickles down to the trenches. I am shocked that our district level point of contact is the person in charge of [a field unrelated to counseling]. They are not the right person to be connecting with the military and sharing information with counselors. *(Counselor, Elementary School)*

According to those we interviewed, educators working with children of Reserve Component soldiers have an even weaker connection with the military. As Reserve Component families are often geographically dispersed, schools serving them may be located far from a military installation. In addition, while the schools near active-duty installations have a military-school liaison, the SLO, who serves at the community level, the USAR or ARNG counterpart, the School Transition Specialist, covers multiple states at once. There are a few notable exceptions, although these tend to be at schools located near a military base or with a larger percentage of military students.[2]

The staff members we interviewed felt unprepared to support children whose parents are deployed due to a perceived disconnection between the Army and Reserve Component families. According to these staff members, typically only the teachers, counselors, and principals who take the initiative to attend training learn about parent deployment and meeting the needs of military children. As a result, many of the school staff members serving the USAR and ARNG families we interviewed were unaware of the potential effects of parent deployment, and even fewer are knowledgeable about the resources available to Reserve Component children and families.

> The education wasn't there on the teachers' part, as far as how to help them or what to do. I guess the teachers didn't realize that there could be an effect on education and behavior when a loved one is deployed. *(Counselor, Middle School)*

> I was not helpful to [one mom] in the beginning because I didn't know she had help that was available. It wasn't until after I went to a training that I learned about the resources available. I didn't know all the services that are available to National Guard families, and I feel like if I had known about these services, I could have been more helpful to the family. *(Counselor, Middle School)*

School staff we interviewed reported that many schools serving Active Component families are also unaware of the range of materials, resources, and services that are available. Those we interviewed who were aware noted that while classes and training are offered, they are not schedule-friendly and not offered often enough. Similarly, the teachers and counselors we interviewed observed that school staff who work with children of Reserve Component soldiers find it difficult to attend training, as they are often held near a military installation.

---

[2]   Since our research was conducted, the Army has added 41 SLOs for a total of 141 Garrison SLOs and has expanded the School Support Program to the Reserve Components and added Reserve SLOs.

Other staff members, serving both Active and Reserve Components, felt the curricula and training sessions are not relevant for the current conflict and situation in schools, do not address how to implement and use the information in the school setting, and are focused primarily on working with and helping the younger children.

> There have been trainings in our state for working with military families, but it hasn't been local, so I haven't been able to go. I would be interested in participating in something like that. I did send for some information . . . but the information I got, I thought it was lacking in the everyday dealing with kids. It wasn't helpful in supporting the kids. *(Counselor, Elementary School)*

> I don't know that their current curriculum reflects the seriousness of the conflict we are in. I don't know if it is specific to elementary kids, not sure about junior high and high school level. Always feel like I am floundering with these kids and I am trying to build relationships, I have a few things up my sleeve but I am not in the military and I don't understand the structure to know what kids are talking about sometimes. *(Counselor, Middle School)*

One program that school staff we interviewed consistently referred to when thinking about positive connections between schools and the military was the "Adopt-A-School" program. Within this program, a unit sends five to ten soldiers to the school once a week to help out with a range of tasks and projects, including helping out in the classroom, moving heavy furniture or equipment, mentoring, or playing with children on the playground. According to those we interviewed, despite the value for the school, as well as the behavioral and emotional health of children whose parents are deployed, frequent and large-scale deployments have made it challenging to sustain the program, although some schools have been able to successfully maintain their "Adopt-A-School" program. School staff members attribute the lasting success to the support of the Sergeant Major and Colonel, who make the program a priority. Staff members noted that "even when the unit was deployed, the rear detachment sent out soldiers so the program never stopped." According to those we interviewed, in addition to the benefit for the children, the soldiers have helped school staff by talking at professional development days about such topics as school engagement with the military. According to those we interviewed, the program has benefits for the soldiers as well, as students and faculty view them as family and regularly send care packages to the units' deployed soldiers.

3.2.3. According to Those We Interviewed, Students May Lose Academic Course Credits and Be Required to Meet New State Requirements When They Transfer from One School District to Another

Some of the challenges that teachers and counselors discussed across groups and locations are ones that stem from the high mobility of this population, which is often amplified during deployment. This and the following findings discuss issues that are primarily relevant to those students that move states when a parent deploys.

While children of military parents are highly mobile in general, schools in both study locations noted that student mobility is more pronounced during parental deployments, as the child may be sent to live with grandparents or other relatives for a period of time, or may move off-post with the nonmilitary parent to be closer to extended family.

School staff we interviewed reported that one challenge with high mobility is that many academic course credits earned by the child do not transfer to his or her new school. School principals and counselors across levels and locations shared that there have been instances in which they try to give the child as many credits as possible for the work they have completed, but also indicated that there may be substantial differences in the quality and requirements for coursework, making it necessary for the child to retake classes or complete additional courses at the new school. This difficulty in transferring credits did not happen for every child, but happened frequently enough to warrant attention.

Teachers in both study sites also reported that the variation in academic requirements and curricula across schools may result in significant knowledge gaps among students. Teachers in middle and high schools noted that these gaps are more pronounced for the older children, as they have experienced a greater number of moves and, at the same time, the coursework and material is more varied and challenging. One counselor noted:

> Students have a lot of academic gaps due to high transfer rate. You really see this over the longer term. *(Counselor, High School)*

Another point of frustration reported by the teachers we interviewed, particularly those of middle and high school students, is that bright students are often not able to take advanced coursework in a given subject because they spend so much time taking or retaking coursework required for graduation or promotion to the next grade. Concern was expressed that the academic trajectory of these children is being altered, and as a result they are not able to realize their full potential due to the time spent meeting the requirements of their new school.

A related concern for the teachers and counselors we interviewed involves state testing. According to those we interviewed, for each move the child makes, he or she must pass the state exam. However, preparation for these tests takes away time and energy students could be spending on other educational objectives. While some states allow a student to waive the test by transferring the child's score from the previous school, school staff across groups and interviews explained that the process does not work efficiently. One staff member shared:

> We have requirements for the [state test]. You can get a waiver, but we wait so long for the waiver and the test results, the child ends up having to take the [test] again. *(Teacher, High School)*

School personnel across school levels and locations were aware of training offered by the military to help with transition issues. Some counselors also reported attending Army-sponsored training such as the Transition Counselors Institute (TCI) and other training offered by the Military Child Education Coalition (MCEC) to improve communication with other schools about transfer issues. However, while the counselors felt that training sessions like these are informative, they struggle with how to translate this information into actionable recommendations, especially when working with students transferring from other states.

3.2.4. School Staff We Interviewed Perceived That Accessing Special Education Services for Recently Transferred Children Is a Tremendous Challenge

While the frequent moves for children of military parents is challenging for a number of reasons, children with special needs are at a particular disadvantage. States vary in their criteria and processes needed to qualify for special education. As a result, according to those we interviewed, with each move to a new state, students often must be reevaluated for special education services. Teachers and counselors across grade levels and study locations reported, however, that a major challenge is that military children do not stay in one place long enough for the problem to be identified or for the children to qualify for services. They also shared that several military children in their school, who may likely qualify for special education services, are not currently receiving them. As one teacher described:

> There needs to be some "stayputedness" to qualify for special education and he has never been in one place long enough to get services. Where to start? We go through transcripts and identify academic holes early on, but as soon as he was identified he moved again. *(Teacher, Middle School)*

One counselor explained that, according to federal law, children do not qualify for special education services if their academic difficulties are due to poor school attendance or poor academic instruction.[3] This is a particular barrier in qualifying military children given their potential for high mobility, extended absences from school, and

---

[3] The Individuals with Disabilities Education Act (IDEA) defines "children with disabilities" as having any of the following types of disabilities: autism, deaf, deaf-blindness, hearing impairments (including deafness), mental retardation, multiple disabilities, orthopedic impairments, other health impairments, serious emotional disturbance, specific learning disabilities, speech or language impairments, traumatic brain injury, and visual impairments (including blindness). It does not include difficulties due to poor attendance or poor academic instruction.

paucity of information regarding the *quality* of instruction received in their former schools. As such, it is much harder to justify special education services for military children.

A final concern raised by teachers and counselors across groups and interviews was that certain states require a doctor's signature in order for the child to qualify for special education services. Teachers and counselors in states where a doctor's signature is required felt that this requirement delays access to needed special education services, particularly when a child has to wait several months before seeing a military doctor. One teacher shared this story:

> I had a child who received special education services in two previous sites that didn't require a doctor's signature. So when they got here, they had to be reevaluated because they had to have a doctor's signature for a 504. The whole process had to start over, even though they had been receiving services for six years. That set that child back a whole year, especially because they had to be seen at [a military hospital], which takes months to get in and now the child is a year behind. [This has] implications for the classroom as they aren't getting extra time, or access to the resource room. *(Teacher, Elementary School)*

3.3. Summary

According to our interviews, while many children appear to be coping well with the challenges of having a deployed parent, other students are facing difficulties related to school engagement, attendance, and transition. Our analysis identifies several factors that appear to contribute to these academic difficulties, including the stress and anxiety of parental absence, disengagement of some nondeployed parents, and difficulty accessing programs or services. Interviews with school staff highlighted the potential effects of parental deployment on a range of outcomes (e.g., attendance, homework, behavioral health) that individually and collectively may influence school success.

CHAPTER FOUR

Behavioral Health Challenges That Children Face When Parents Deploy

---

In Chapter Three we discussed the impact that parental deployment can have on the academic success of the child. The teachers, counselors, and MFLCs we interviewed reported that often, when a child struggled with deployment, they would link the issues and academic challenges to underlying psychological and behavioral health issues of both students and their nondeployed parents. As a result of the perceived psychological health issues facing some nondeployed parents, staff felt that the burden is increasingly falling on the teachers, counselors, and staff of the school. Yet they do not feel they have adequate training or assistance to help these students. For children of Guard and Reserve soldiers, providing support is even more challenging. Further, the need for this support does not end when the parent comes home. Reintegration introduces a new set of issues, dynamics, and concerns for many students and their family members.

This chapter first describes the perspectives of teachers, counselors, and school administrators regarding the impact of parental deployments on the psychological and behavioral health functioning of children and their nondeployed parents. We then provide background on some of the behavioral health service options available to these families. We examine some of these behavioral health issues that were first articulated by school staff from the perspective of providers, insurers, MFLCs, and other behavioral health experts. It is important to note that our analysis focuses solely on the perspectives of the school staff and providers that we interviewed. We have not sought to validate these perceptions through more objective measures, nor are we able to determine the extent to which challenges and barriers in services that they identify as stemming from parental deployment may also be ascribed to challenges in the civilian health care sector, schools more broadly, or children with behavioral health needs more broadly.

4.1. Student Functioning and Behavioral Health Issues of the Child and Parent

4.1.1. Academic Outcomes May Be Affected by a Child's Poor Emotional Health During Multiple and Extended Deployments

Our interviews revealed that a complete understanding of student academic challenges during deployments requires a detailed exploration of how concurrent psychological and behavioral health issues of parents and students can impede academic success. According to school members we interviewed, while some students are able to address successfully the challenges introduced from parental deployment, many are struggling with these periods of separation.

School staff across grade levels and study locations shared that students are unclear about when their parent will leave home, or when he or she will return. This lack of understanding may engender fear about losing a parent or anxiety about the parent at home, which may result in classroom behavior problems, and may have a subsequent negative impact on academic performance. Further, the uncertainty surrounding deployment extensions may contribute to the anxiety experienced by students. The deployments may impact a child's mood, leading to sadness and anger. For example, teachers we interviewed observed that some children may hold anger that ultimately disrupts classroom activity or peer relationships in school. Further, counselors noted that children often reflect the psychological health of their parent. Thus, when a parent is upset, the child may experience sadness as well. One staff member shared:

> Children are little barometers—they pick up on however mom or dad is feeling and they bring that to school. They'll carry the

anger with them to school. Or sadness. If it's chaotic at home, there's a lot more hostility and impulsiveness that comes in to school. *(Teacher, Elementary School)*

The school staff we interviewed perceived important gender differences in how the deployment impact manifests; for boys, anger and aggression are more common, while for girls, internalizing behaviors such as depression are prevalent. In some of the focus groups, staff shared that girls are "frequent flyers" and visit the school nurse with somatic complaints of stomachaches, headache, and general malaise. A few school leaders shared concerns that middle and high school age female students are engaging in other health risk-taking behaviors, including cutting and promiscuous sexual behavior. Many school leaders in these groups traced these emotional difficulties to the absence of the father, which can disrupt the household routine and family functioning. One teacher explained:

If a kid is acting out, we involve the parent and that is when you find out that a parent is deployed. It makes a big difference when dad is gone as far as behavior and academics. Plus, boys are more disruptive, girls are more emotional, withdrawn, and really worried. *(Counselor, Middle School)*

Moms need help. They say that they don't know what to do. [They tell me] "Anything I try just doesn't work. He is too big to discipline. I have no idea what to do with him. I wish I could help you but I can't." *(Counselor, Middle School)*

In some instances, school staff felt that the acting-out behaviors may be a veiled plea for attention when children are seeking some parental involvement.

We had a kid last year who was constantly in trouble. And his dad kept coming up here, every time he got in trouble. It turned out that the kid was doing it purposely to get his dad's attention—even bad attention—before he left. *(Teacher, Middle School)*

There also seem to be important age differences in how these emotional difficulties are revealed. The feelings of middle school students, who are already dealing with rapid emotional and physical changes, are compounded during deployment. Staff members in middle schools across study locations shared that these students may need options to redirect their frustrations. On the other hand, younger students often do not have the cognitive abilities to understand exactly what is occurring. For example, these students might confuse a 15-month deployment with 15 days.

> I notice that children who are young just really miss them [their deployed parent], they think they are gone and don't grasp that they are coming back. *(Counselor, Elementary School)*

The MFLCs we interviewed confirmed staff reports of the psychological and behavioral health challenges of students. MFLCs noted that while they do help children address issues related to deployment, reintegration, and separation, they also help children deal with many day-to-day issues.

> Because their anxiety is heightened their ability to deal with the day-to-day stuff is harder.

MFLCs also noted that many children are worried and experience stress about their parent in combat. They also felt, in many cases, that resiliency was waning among children experiencing multiple deployments.

> While people think that children find multiple deployments easier, they don't, they get harder. Their parent is on third, fourth, fifth deployment and they are tired of it. Also depends on casualties in parent's unit. If hearing of a lot of injuries, casualties, they are obviously more scared.

MFLCs reported that they observe parental conflict, which translates into stress for the children. In addition to worrying about the safety of their deployed parent, children may confront the potential that their parents will separate or divorce, even when one parent is still deployed.

Finally, similar to staff reports, MFLCs also noted that parental involvement in schools is a significant challenge.

> This school has more parents who are less involved. They have a lot of stress, mental health issues.

> We had a meeting about school testing and not one parent came to learn about it, we held one in morning and one at night and no one came. Parents are not coming out even though they say they will come. I don't know if/how the MFLC program could motivate parents because we often get the "we don't need counseling," but it is really support.

4.1.2. Staff Members We Interviewed Reported That Some Parents Struggle More Than Their Children with Deployments

The teachers and counselors across groups and interviews perceived that many of the academic challenges were linked to underlying psychological and behavioral health issues. In addition to student psychological and behavioral health issues, staff members observed that parental psychological and behavioral health and the changing home life also may underlie many of the challenges that students face during these multiple and extended deployments. Several respondents across groups and interviews shared that some parents are experiencing depression, which is a tremendous stressor on children who are anxious or worried about their parents. These depressed parents may not engage with the school sufficiently, missing meetings with teachers, not bringing children to school activities, and not ensuring that children are completing homework. Further, staff members across groups and interviews reported that some parents keep children out of school as a source of comfort to them during the deployment (i.e., not wanting to be separated from their child).

Lot of parents—it is hard to get up and even take a shower. Kids don't come to school because that is someone they [parents] can hold on to. *(Teacher, Elementary School)*

Teachers across grade levels and study locations also noted that boys are often worried or concerned about a situation at home, because they are now the "man of the house" and need to take care of their mother and siblings.

The boys are told, "I am going away and you are going to be the man of the house, and you are going to have to help your mother." They don't realize when they say it, but that is a lot of stress on kids. *(Counselor, Middle School)*

Staff members reported that children can become the emotional partners of their home caregiver, which also places undue burden and stress on their lives. For example, these students are worried about their parents' marriage or relationship both during and after deployment as well as their home caregiver's psychological health. Staff members across groups and interviews reported that some students share their anxieties with them about helping their caregiver when their mother or father is deployed.

Students have big roles to fill, are confidants of parents. They are shouldering adult issues, know of affairs, relationship issues between parents. They are concerned about parents. *(Teacher, Middle School)*

Staff members also reported that some parents are relying too heavily on their children for emotional support, even young children. One teacher described:

Parents confiding with kids, confiding with their rock, but their rock is five years old. *(Teacher, Elementary School)*

When the home caregiver is depressed or unable to handle the deployment well and the other parent is away, many children are left without parental supervision or support.

If the mother's not used to having the father gone, the mothers get depressed, and the kids aren't getting support from their mom anymore. It's like double jeopardy—their dad's gone and their mom might as well be gone. *(Counselor, Elementary School)*

Staff members in the groups shared that some parents are stressed to the point of anxiety and communicating with them can be challenging. Interacting with these parents when they do come to the school can be difficult.

I see the parents stressed out, when I talk to them. No matter what you say, they aren't hearing you. So you just listen and try to get some positive words out, but it is tough. *(Counselor, Middle School)*

4.1.3. According to School Staff We Interviewed, Although Deployments Are Becoming a Routine Part of Children's Lives, for Many Children, Resiliency Appears to Be Waning

School staff across all grade levels and study locations reported that many children are displaying exceptional resiliency in the face of the deployments. Staff members shared that although there may be a decline in academic performance when the parent is initially deployed, these children are able to organize themselves to perform well in the future. For instance, some students have learned skills from the first deployment that have strengthened their abilities to cope and function well for the subsequent deployments. One teacher remarked:

I have seen kids go from totally lost after the first round of deployment to picking themselves up and living day-to-day. It becomes a new normal. *(Teacher, Elementary School)*

While the deployments have been normalized or routinized to an extent for some students, most staff noted that the resiliency to these events is not what it once was for many other children and families. In addition to the changes in the individual experience of students, staff members reported that there have been transformations in the school environment response to the deployments. In the first years of the war, there was more anxiety in classrooms about what was occurring, but now the response in the classroom is more subdued and seen as usual life.

Staff observed that the ability of children to confront the parental separations with the same emotional resolve has been hampered by the extended and multiple deployments. In the groups and interviews, school staff noted that some students have become more apathetic to the upcoming deployment; one teacher noted that these children have "become calloused" to the deployment. A counselor shared:

> The resiliency in family has been used up. In the beginning there was a lot of pride, and then talking about being there a long time, but families that used to be able to get kids to school on time cannot do it anymore. *(Counselor, Middle School)*

4.1.4. Staff Reported That Schools May Be Becoming a Stable Place or Sanctuary for Students When Home Life Is Chaotic or Uncertain

School staff of younger children also reported that they struggle with how emotionally needy some children are when their parent is deployed. While teachers are willing to help their students, those serving a large proportion of military students find the situation overwhelming at times.

> I have never felt so taxed as I have this year. I have never felt so much negativity and frustration and I don't know what to do. I am struggling emotionally because of it. Kids are more needy and sucking it out of us. *(Teacher, Elementary School)*

Staff members across grade levels and study locations reported that students often stay at school for long periods after school has ended because the school is seen as a "safe place" for engaging with teachers and peers, and allows them to limit their time at home. Teachers who referenced these student issues also shared that some children have great need for attention, and in a few instances the students referred to school staff members as "daddy and mom." This neediness takes time to address and ultimately detracts from academic instruction.

I had one girl who was very clingy and very needy. I finally had to tell her, "You can have two hugs a day, and you can't leave a class to get a hug." This was right after her dad left. She was just so needy. She's a little better about it now. *(Teacher, Elementary School)*

Staff members across groups and interviews also cited an increasing demand for after-school activities for these youth because some students would prefer to stay at school rather than go home. School staff shared that some parents may also benefit from their child participating in these activities, given that parents may work or have other household obligations to attend to and may need some additional child care coverage. One challenge, however, concerns the ability of schools to extend their day and to have the resources and staff to maintain this programming. Staff felt that the lack of transportation home after the school activities would make it difficult for some children to regularly attend, again citing work schedules and responsibilities of the nondeployed parent.

4.1.5. Staff Members We Interviewed Perceived That Some Students, Particularly Those Whose Parents Are in the Reserve Component, May Feel Isolated

As USAR and ARNG soldiers are often not clustered around a military installation, the teachers and counselors we interviewed reported that students whose parents are deployed with the Reserve Component may not have peers with whom they can share their experiences. In addition, most of the teachers and counselors we interviewed who were working with Reserve Component families had only one or two such students in their school, and many noted that those students did not know any other Reserve Component families. Under these conditions, having a parent deploy may be an extremely isolating experience for a child. One counselor who is also a National Guard member said:

They feel like they're the only ones who feel like that—that they're going crazy. [Parent deployment] needs to be normalized . . . I think that is the key thing that's missing. It is an issue with

National Guard because we are all spread out. *(Counselor, Middle School)*

Some of the school staff members serving USAR and ARNG described living in supportive communities where churches, local business, and other organizations held special events for military families. Other communities were less supportive, and a hostile environment may intensify a child's feeling of isolation. These staff observed that general community environment may affect children's feelings of isolation.

Kids might be feeling uncomfortable admitting that they have a parent who is in the military because of an antiwar sentiment by teachers or others. At the same time, many of them are very proud of a parent serving. *(Administrator)*

4.1.6. School Staff Noted That the Reintegration of the Service Member Can Be Challenging for the Family Unit

Reintegration, when the service member returns home, may also be a difficult time for families. While school staff shared that students generally expressed excitement to have their mother or father back home, these reunions may be very challenging and disruptive to the new dynamic that has been created in that parent's absence. School staff noted that some children struggle with relating to the deployed parent again and any changes in his or her mood, as well as determining which adult is setting household rules. In addition, children may feel left out when parents are also trying to reunite themselves.

Parents who return say "don't talk to me right now, we'll talk about it later" but later never comes. The kids lose their relationship with their parent during the deployment and it takes so long for the parent to readjust, that by the time they get adjusted, the kid is already used to it [not having the parent available]. *(Counselor, Middle School)*

The return can be the most traumatic—more traumatic than the deployment itself. There is a certain amount of normalcy in the deployment; although a parent's absence creates a disruption, this disruption is similar to other disruptions that could occur, like during weekend training. At the return, however, everyone has changed because of time passing and experiences. Their presence now is an unavoidable conflict. Some people describe that as the crisis more than any other time. *(Administrator)*

School staff across grade levels and study locations shared that some students who have experienced multiple deployments are not adjusting well with the separations and returns, which is revealed in the classroom.

They [students] also expect more attention when the parent returns, but if they don't get it, then they don't understand what is happening. They're confused, and they come to school, and don't know how to express their confusion. That's when you get defiance. *(Counselor, Middle School)*

4.2. Barriers to Addressing Child Psychological and Behavioral Health Needs

Since the teachers and counselors discussed the relationship between academic functioning and behavioral health, we endeavored to briefly examine some of the formal behavioral health services that may be available to their students and families and the challenges, if any, that exist to helping families gain access to these services. We acknowledge that there is a broad range of behavioral or emotional issues cited by school staff to explain some of the academic difficulties, but this investigation primarily focused on the formal services that may be useful for students and families dealing with the more difficult issues. We examine barriers to receiving behavioral health services as identified by TRICARE insurers and behavioral health providers. It should be noted that many of the issues raised by the providers serving military youth are critical challenges for the civilian sector, namely availability of providers and adequate geographic distribution of services. Themes that were shared by stakeholders are noted broadly. If an issue was only raised by one stakeholder, that too is noted. The issues shared by providers inform recommendations for service improvement and expansion in Chapter Five.

Most of the providers and insurers we interviewed felt that there had been an increase in the number of youths needing behavioral or psychological health services since 2002, though this was anecdotal and perspectives varied. Although there have been studies since data collection for this study was completed that have documented increases in insurance claims for behavioral health services (Gorman, Eide, and Hisle-Gorman, 2010), our analysis primarily focuses on the perception of change in the number of children and adolescents seen and the increase in the severity of the issues. For instance, providers described an increase in the number of children and adolescents who are severely disturbed and more challenges among younger children. Several believed that the impact of deployment on families has been worse than during prior wars.

Some providers also shared concerns about older children, including a rise in depression, more referrals for substance-use problems, and increases in adjustment disorders. A few providers described their perceptions of increases in eating disorders and cutting among girls, and more "acting out" or conduct issues among both girls and boys.

Overall, these providers felt that children of different ages respond differently to the stages of the deployment cycle. For example, deployments may be more difficult for younger children, but reintegration may create more challenges with children in middle or later childhood. Leave, where the parent returns home from deployment for a short period, can be stressful for children and youth as they adjust to having their deployed parent home for only a short time.

4.2.1. According to the Stakeholders We Interviewed, the Number of Available Providers with Training in Child and Adolescent Services Is Low

A common refrain from providers and, to a lesser extent, the contractors under TRICARE who felt that the issue was being addressed more readily at the time of data collection, was a concern about the number of psychological and behavioral health providers available to serve children and youth, especially the youngest children (0–5 years of age). Ensuring that families have timely access to behavioral or psychological health services for children can be challenging, particularly when there is a national shortage in psychological and behavioral health providers. Further, the number of providers who have specific training in child and adolescent development is much smaller. The issue of provider supply has been a challenge plaguing the civilian and military sectors of the behavioral health system. For instance, the number of child and adolescent psychiatry training programs nationally has decreased from 130 programs in 1980 to 114 programs in 2002 (Koppelman, 2004). The National Task Force on Child and Adolescent Psychiatry estimated in 2003 that, given the growing child psychological and behavioral health need, we would need 12,624 child and adolescent psychiatrists in 2020 but would only have 8,312 available if training trends continued (Kim, 2003). A recent study of military psychologists and psychiatrists specifically also shows a decline in provider availability; in 2007–2008, the Army had only 13 psychology interns, when 36 could have been accepted (Department of Defense Task Force on Mental Health, 2007).

In addition to the absolute shortage, there is wide geographic variation in provider availability (Kim, 2003), a finding that holds for Army installations as well. A survey by Russell et al. (2008) reported that 22 of 30 Army catchment areas have shortages in child and adolescent psychiatry services based on the numbers of youth and estimated need. According to this analysis, Fort Sam Houston and Fort Leavenworth had the greatest number of child psychiatrists (31.0 and 41.9 per 100,000 military youth, respectively) and Fort Bragg, Fort Lewis (now JBLM), Fort Campbell, and Fort Hood all have more than 20,000 youth in excess of the capacity of Child and Adolescent Psychiatry Services (CAPS) (Russell et al., 2008).

Providers noted that some families become frustrated with long wait times to schedule initial and follow-up appointments for their children. While the availability of behavioral health service phone lines helped families find a provider quickly, many providers continued to be concerned about the inability of families to access timely services.

A related challenge discussed by stakeholders is that many civilian providers do not accept TRICARE and that reimbursement rates in certain geographic locations made it difficult to attract and retain these psychiatrists. This may be of particular concern for activated ARNG or USAR families or families enrolled in TRICARE Reserve Select, who may be less connected to military health providers.

While there are limits on the numbers of psychiatrists, especially in remote areas or areas with fewer psychiatrists overall, some providers argued that one of the key problems in provider capacity is the fact that the available child and adolescent psychiatrists must often spend time treating adults, rather than youth. According to the providers we interviewed, this issue may be due to the increase in psychological and behavioral health needs among returning service members, along with the low availability of nondeployed psychological and behavioral health professionals available to treat individuals in need.

While psychiatrists may be an important component of the total behavioral health provider workforce, providers and insurers noted that diversity in the provider base, including clinical psychologists, clinical social workers, and marriage and family therapists, is also important. They suggested continuing to expand training programs for these types of providers in order to address growing youth psychological and behavioral health need. TRICARE contractors discussed the importance of using their network social workers, licensed marriage and family therapists, and pastoral providers. However, they contended that often the first request or referral from primary care providers is for psychiatric services.

Providers and insurers also shared that availability and coverage of certain behavioral or psychological health services is not adequate in terms of addressing appropriate treatment requirements. While there have been tremendous improvements in the coverage for behavioral or psychological health services under TRICARE, providers and insurers described concerns about continued gaps in services. One critical area raised almost universally was the lack of availability of residential treatment facilities. Many facilities are not fully or appropriately certified, thus providers often must refer families to residential treatment centers outside of the state. In addition, providers argued that the intermediate step between outpatient care and residential care (e.g., some form of inpatient services) is often difficult to access. Further, providers related that continuity of care between an inpatient hospitalization and home services for those with more serious emotional issues needs improvement. As mentioned above, there are also particular challenges related to substance-use services and treatment as admission to inpatient facilities primarily for rehabilitation is generally not authorized and *individual* outpatient therapy is typically not covered for substance-use disorders.

Despite advances in creating individualized treatment plans, according to providers, many of the services remain fragmented, making it difficult for children facing multiple needs and providers (e.g., social worker, developmental specialist, psychiatrist) to have a coordinated care plan. Stakeholders also reported challenges in coordinating wraparound services, which include a comprehensive array of home, school, or community-based professional services individualized to meet a child's needs.

According to the providers we interviewed, other services that are not sufficiently covered or available include in-home services and treatment for eating disorders. For example, one provider described an instance when she had to refer a patient to the U.S. mainland because there were no adequate eating disorder facilities in Hawaii. In addition, even if family-based services are covered by TRICARE, providers shared that they do not conduct much family-based counseling because of the provider shortage and overall limits in time to pursue this treatment modality. Finally, the psychological and behavioral health professionals we interviewed noted that there is not enough respite care for parents and families of particularly troubled children, and that this stress may have an undue impact on the children as well if not addressed.

4.2.2. Some Civilian Providers May Need Help Understanding Military Culture

Another issue shared by the providers we interviewed is a lack of experience with military culture and with problems that are particular to the military and deployment. These providers indicated that while many of the providers who see TRICARE patients have current or prior military experience, newer providers to this community may not have as much understanding of the unique needs of military families. Behavioral health providers who primarily serve civilian populations may be relatively new to the issues and concerns of military families. The TRICARE contractors we interviewed described the need for more training opportunities for these providers as well as orienting providers to military support services, such as Military OneSource. Such efforts could increase provider awareness about the most salient issues potentially affecting children and families during deployment.

4.2.3. The Stakeholders We Interviewed Reported That Availability of Prevention, Screening, and Early Intervention Varies Widely Across the United States

Many providers described the need to emphasize more the prevention, improved screening, and early detection of behavioral or psychological health needs. For example, one provider shared:

> My mission is to help the world understand that the answer to behavioral and emotional needs is not going to be done by hiring child psychiatrists and psychologists. Teaching residents about primary prevention is the model we need to use.

In the area of screening and early intervention, providers reported that there has been some improvement in schools and in primary care settings. However, interviewees argued for more attention to psychological and behavioral health issues in these settings to address the needs of the child before they become more severe and require the services of child and adolescent psychiatrists specifically. It should be noted that this challenge is not specific to the military; prevention is a concern for the broader student body as well, and schools struggle with integrating behavioral health support in schools.

School psychological and behavioral health services have increased over the last several years in the general population, and this approach is now being used to serve military youth. Some, but not all, of the providers we interviewed shared successes of clinical and prevention services being provided to military children in the schools. The schools are natural settings for addressing youth psychological and behavioral health needs given the length of time children spend in school and the ability to decrease stigma associated with seeking services (Hoover et al., 2007). Plus, given the shortage in providers, conducting services and, in particular, group therapy in schools may be an additional resource to address these gaps in care. Currently in the Army there are School Behavioral Health Programs at JBLM, Schofield Barracks, Fort Campbell, Fort Meade, Bavaria, Baumholder, and Fort Carson.

Despite this focus of moving behavioral health support services into schools, some providers requested more guidance on how to establish services in schools, including how to create relationships with school staff and effectively sustain the link between identifying a student with a need and providing appropriate and continuous services within the school and/or clinical setting. One provider expressed concern that some of the school-based programs were well-intentioned, but those providing services may not have the required clinical training to implement these services effectively or respond to student concerns appropriately.

In addition to increasing services in schools, all providers argued for greater focus on psychological and behavioral health in primary care settings. This is a not a new approach, as the civilian sector has been grappling with this issue for some time (New Freedom Commission, 2003; Ginsburg, 2008). Co-locating primary and behavioral services and equipping primary care providers with basic psychological and behavioral health screening skills addresses some of the difficulty in obtaining specialty psychological and behavioral health services that families face (National Institute for Health Care Management, 2009). Further, these methods can counter the fact that patients do not always recognize when they have a psychological or behavioral health issue. Providers recommended placing behavioral health resource information in primary care office settings where families can obtain services without stigma and access issues that families may face when trying to navigate multiple provider locations.

Providers and insurers also described specific concerns that the needs of preschool children may be missed, given the fact that younger children are less connected to schools, where academic or behavioral challenges may be identified by school personnel. The providers we spoke with contended that the needs of younger children are also often missed because pediatricians are not necessarily screening young children for psychological and behavioral health issues, as they may do for their adolescent population, where such issues are more prevalent.

4.2.4. School Staff Members We Interviewed Reported That Schools May Not Have Adequate Assistance in Helping Students and Parents Access Psychological and Behavioral Health Services

School leaders requested that more effort be placed on providing linkage assistance for obtaining psychological and behavioral health services. Counselors across schools, in particular, discussed how often they attempted to provide referrals to students and families only to learn about extended wait times and difficulties navigating the psychological and behavioral health care system. These staff members explained that up-to-date referral lists of available providers within a defined region are needed to let families know where to obtain services for child psychological and behavioral health screening and services. One counselor described:

> The military is getting better at taking care of soldiers with counseling, etc., but they seem to have forgotten about the families. *(Counselor, Elementary School)*

The counselors across grade levels and study locations also explained that a differentiation between academic counselor and psychosocial counselor is needed. In most public schools, counselors are often unable to address the psychological and behavioral health needs of students given the academic mandates that they must follow. Counselors we interviewed felt a good design would be for the military to support a full-time psychological and behavioral health counselor who could work with the academic counselors currently in the schools, and who would have a set schedule, dividing his or her time between several schools in the area. This would allow children to be seen by a counselor with direct knowledge and expertise related to deployments, bring additional expertise to the school regarding military life and deployments, and alleviate some of the burden currently experienced by school staff that is created by parental deployment. One staff member shared:

> We are a band-aid entity, so to speak, but it is extremely frustrating when families need to address these issues. We need time to confront these issues. They need an outlet, and we could do a lot in the school. (*Teacher, Middle School*)

4.2.5. The Providers We Interviewed Reported That Engagement of Families in Psychological and Behavioral Health Services and Education About These Services May Be Challenging

According to most providers, engaging families in behavioral health services was somewhat difficult. One provider shared that even when services are available and offered, some families "just don't see the problem." Further, the stigma associated with using these services is still a barrier, though providers argued that most parents were more willing to seek services for their children than for themselves.

In addition to the continuing negative attitudes or stigma associated with psychological and behavioral health services, providers shared that it can be problematic to engage families in services over time. This issue resulted primarily from logistic challenges (e.g., transportation, ability to get an appointment at a time that is convenient) and the level of priority the family placed on behavioral or psychological health treatment compared to the myriad of practical issues that they needed to address during deployment.

Finally, providers shared that one of the key issues that insurers confront is educating families about when they need to access formal psychological and behavioral health services versus using online or community support services. These insurers felt that some of the online tools, such as Military OneSource, could assist families in making informed decisions about behavioral health options. In addition, some providers discussed the difficulty in explaining to families the importance of early intervention and other services that may help to prevent their child's psychological or behavioral issue from becoming more severe.

4.2.6. MFLC Integration into Schools Can Be Challenging and Frequent Rotations May Undermine Continuity

The MFLC program is broadly designed to provide support and assistance to soldiers in the Active and Reserve Components, military family members, and civilian personnel. MFLCs can serve as a much-needed resource to students, families, and school staff. MFLCs not only provide training and information to teachers, counselors, and administrative staff about military life, culture, and the impact that parental deployment may have on children, but they also can provide specific strategies to help teachers better support a struggling student in the classroom.

Although MFLCs are housed in schools, they are not considered school staff. The program was specifically designed in this way to enhance student and parent comfort and address issues of stigma. Services are confidential and anonymous and are not linked to either the military or the schools. For students and families, MFLCs provide nonmedical consultation, that is, they do not provide therapy or counseling; if therapy is needed the student or family is referred out. MFLCs work with students on an individual basis to develop strategies and tools that the student can use to overcome his or her current challenges (e.g., high levels of stress, worry, sadness, anger). There are currently 158 MFLCs in schools across the country.

MFLCs reported that schools overall seem to be very enthusiastic about their presence. According to the MFLCs we interviewed, the main challenge for schools is the transition to having their first MFLC rotation, as staff may not seem to fully understand the role of the MFLC or the ways in which the MFLC could support students, families, and school staff. MFLCs did note that by the end of the first rotation, staff had a much better understanding and began to use the MFLC as a resource and refer children in need; however, integration can be slow. One MFLC noted that sites and schools often do not understand the MFLC program well enough to make the best use of this resource:

> Principal might get notified [that we are coming], but no one else, it doesn't seem to trickle down so kids are not referred and

teachers don't use us as much. We come in and do a briefing but that may be the first time they hear of it and it takes a while for teachers to use us. But particularly for new schools, there needs to be more systematic dissemination of information before we get there; that would make it easier for us to do our job. When you're new, you're not used as effectively.

Another issue raised by every MFLC we interviewed was the rotation schedule. MFLCs are in schools for approximately three months, generally following the academic calendar. The first rotation may be from the start of school to winter break, for example, the second from early January to spring break, and the third from spring break to the end of school. The MFLCs we interviewed noted that schools often ask them to stay for the full year to maintain continuity and continue with the work they started. While MFLCs acknowledged that there may be a benefit to longer rotations, they also noted that they understood why rotations were short. MFLCs are not school staff, and the concern is that if they stay for a full academic year, students, families, and school staff may start to see them as part of the school. This may affect the willingness of students and families to request help. The "outside" presence and short stays allowed MFLCs to observe schools and attend to the needs of the students without those biases. MFLCs noted that this is a continual tension, and they can see advantages and disadvantages to both rotation schedules.

> Right now I am doing a three-month rotation. By the second month, teachers were referring more kids to me. I am getting started and then getting ready to leave. That is pretty typical for the program. A lot of school people would want us there for at least a full school year. But they don't want us to be part of the school staff. It may be easier for people to talk to us, since we are not part of the system. It is a tension.

According to the MFLCs we interviewed, continuity of service, given the short rotation schedule, may be further challenged because records are not kept on the students or their progress. This lack of records and written notes ensures confidentiality but also may preclude a rigorous assessment of effectiveness and accountability. Continuity in services requires a warm handoff from the former to the new MFLC, where the student's situation and effective strategies for supporting that student are discussed verbally. The extent to which all information is captured during this process is not clear, or whether the student and family would be better served if such information could be transmitted via written notes.

4.2.7. The MFLCs We Interviewed Also Noted the Challenge of Tracking the Progress and Impact of the Program

Our interviews revealed the benefits of structuring a program that was short-term and relied on the MFLC "outside" presence to overcome many of the stigma-related barriers associated with behavioral health services. However, the MFLCs we interviewed noted that the lack of any real monitoring and evaluation of services makes it exceedingly difficult to assess whether and how the program is having a positive impact on youth and families. MFLC respondents noted that it would be useful to monitor if and how families connect to formal behavioral health services and whether the program is having a positive impact on youth and families.

Overall, providers and insurers highlighted a number of challenges and gaps for military children related to prevention and early intervention, accessing treatment, continuity of care, and the mode and location of service delivery. In Chapter Five we provide recommendations for how the Army and the civilian sector (primarily schools) may continue to support military children before, during, and after parental deployment.

Recommendations

Our analysis highlights several possible challenges and barriers faced by military children before, during, and after parental deployment for further investigation. In this chapter we propose recommended steps the Army might take to address these challenges and barriers, while acknowledging that additional analyses are needed to understand their scope and severity. In general, our recommendations are intended for military leaders, but we acknowledge that full implementation of many of these recommendations requires enhancing the partnership between schools, behavioral health providers, and the Army to address these issues jointly. Further, since the start of our study, there has already been momentum toward implementing many of these recommendations. However, the ongoing deployments and the academic and behavioral health needs identified in this study suggest that continued vigilance and attention to the broad array of policy and program strategies to address these needs is merited.

Where available, we also provide information on potential military and civilian models related to those strategies that may be referenced as sources for lessons learned. Given that many of these models have not undergone a rigorous evaluation, they should be considered as starting points from which the Army can build and evaluate tailored solutions to academic and behavioral health needs.

Our goal in providing these recommendations is to give the Army and interested communities suggestions for how to address specific challenges or barriers we identified, but our study was not designed as a program gap analysis. Rather, our recommendations stem from study analyses and are fairly general, thus leaving the specific program design elements to be developed under the familiar policy limitations of budget constraints, feasibility constraints, and local implementation issues. In several recommendation areas, we note that activities are under way in both the Army and civilian sectors, thus our recommendations seek to lend further support for those efforts. In other recommendation areas, we offer suggestions for expansion or targeting of services.

Most of these recommendations come with financial costs, and in some cases these costs are likely to be considerable. Where possible, we comment on the relative cost implications of the approaches we present; estimating the costs of each of these possibilities, however, is outside the scope of our analysis. Therefore, we offer them as recommendations for the Army to *consider*, as our analysis suggests that there could be benefits from implementation. But before the Army pursues any of these changes, we recommend a careful analysis of the costs and likely benefits associated with them.

In the next sections we describe recommendations that emerged from our analysis of the academic and school-based needs of children of deployed parents, and recommendations that emerged from our analysis of behavioral health issues. These recommendations stem directly from the findings from our interviews with school staff and behavioral health care specialists and stakeholders, so we briefly summarize those findings here.

As presented in Chapter Three, according to the school teachers, counselors, and administrative staff we interviewed, some children of deployed soldiers may face a number of academic and school-related challenges. Children may struggle with homework completion and attendance, particularly if academic performance is not a priority of the nondeployed parent or if the child has taken on additional household responsibilities. Parental deployment may also precipitate the relocation of the family to another state, and this, according to those we interviewed, can add other academic challenges related to mobility such as difficulty transferring course credits, spending additional time meeting different state requirements, and for some children, qualifying for special services. School staff also felt that they did not have adequate information about the military and deployment status of the parents of the children at the school, or about how best to help children and families who are struggling with parental deployment. Table 5.1 maps the correspondence between the finding areas and recommendations for academic challenges that children face when parents deploy.

In Chapter Four we presented the behavioral health challenges that providers and teachers reported some children face when their parents deploy and the barriers to their receiving care as identified by those we interviewed. Many of the concerns that school staff shared were focused on social and emotional needs of their students, rather than simply academic concerns. The teachers and providers we interviewed identified barriers to addressing child behavioral health needs, including: a low availability of and training for providers, low and variable availability of prevention, screening, and early intervention in many locations, challenges in connecting families with services either because school staff are not familiar with those services or because they

Table 5.1
Academic Challenges and Barriers with Corresponding Recommendations

Challenges and Barriers		Recommendations
3.1. Student academic challenges	5.1.1:	Provide military resources to support students with their schoolwork
	5.1.2:	Develop a set of procedures for schools to use in seeking Army Community Services (ACS) support
	5.1.3:	Consider increasing transportation services for youth
	5.1.4:	Advocate for full adoption and prompt, effective implementation of the Interstate Compact on Educational Opportunity for Military Children
3.2. Barriers to addressing child academic needs	5.1.5:	Develop methods to inform schools about which children are military and about parental deployments
	5.1.6:	Expand efforts to educate school staff members about the military
	5.1.7:	Provide staff with a way to access information on military support and services available to families
	5.1.8:	Improve the presence of the School Liaison Officer (SLO) and enhance collaboration between SLOs and schools
	5.1.9:	Revitalize the "Adopt-A-School" program

have trouble engaging the family in accessing them, challenges in evaluating and monitoring of MFLCs while maintaining their "outside" presence, and a social isolation that some Reserve and Guard families and particularly youth may feel in areas with few other military families. Interviews with school staff and with behavioral health specialists including MFLCs provided context for these issues and support for associated program recommendations. Table 5.2 maps the correspondence between the finding areas and recommendations for behavioral health challenges that children face when parents deploy.

Although the Army has numerous support programs in place for military children, these recommendations address possible gaps in service that remain as well as the needs of families and schools to maximize support services to children and promote academic success. These recommendations are intended for the Army, the school districts, and other youth service providers.

Table 5.2
Behavioral Health Challenges and Barriers with Corresponding Recommendations

Issues and Barriers	Recommendations
4.1 and 4.2. Student functioning and behavioral health issues and barriers to addressing child behavioral health needs	5.2.1: Continue to build psychological and behavioral health service capacity by increasing the number of military counselors
	5.2.2: Expand provider training on military culture and potential impact of deployment
	5.2.3: Continue to expand models for improving access for hard-to-reach or remote youth populations, including telepsychiatry and promoting social networks among Reserve Component families and children
	5.2.4: Enhance integration of behavioral health services with primary care
	5.2.5: Augment school health services for military youth and families
	5.2.6: Improve family engagement in behavioral health services
	5.2.7: Provide school staff with up-to-date information on military and community behavioral health services
	5.2.8: Improve evaluation of the MFLC program by integrating some outcomes-based measurement

5.1. Recommendations to Address Academic and School-Based Needs of Children of Deployed Parents

Teachers and counselors report that some children of deployed parents struggled with homework completion and school attendance, often because teachers believe parents were disengaged from school or because the child had to take on additional home responsibilities. Teachers reported that participation in after-school activities can also be a challenge when the nondeployed parent is struggling with the deployment of the other parent, but these activities can be an important outlet and source of support for these children.

Recommendation 5.1.1: Provide additional resources to support students with their schoolwork, particularly during parental deployment or before and after extended absences from school due to parental R&R.

School staff with whom we spoke felt that one of the biggest academic challenges facing children of deployed parents is the lack of homework completion. Although schools have expressed a willingness to work with children and families to maintain the children's academic trajectories, steps should be taken to expand the academic and homework support provided to military children and to promote distance learning when it is not possible for them to be in school for extended periods of time.

This may include supporting after-school tutors or resource room personnel either on post or at the school, or purchasing monthly online homework help for military children, which can be used at varying times of the day or week.[1] The costs associated with this support will vary widely depending on specific program elements, such as the level and frequency of support and the physical resources (trailers or buildings for personal tutoring support, number of computers for online support) that are provided.

---

[1]   Many installations have after-school programs, including tutoring, but this has not been formalized.

The Army has already implemented Study Strong (via Tutor.com) online tutoring services, which provide individualized online tutoring support on a wide range of subjects. Access to a service such as this would be useful to children of deployed soldiers in a variety of capacities. It could help a child prepare for or catch up from a long absence associated with deployment, including block leave, and could also help support a child who is struggling academically while a parent is deployed. Finally, it could help smooth a child's academic transition to another state. While teachers and counselors work to provide these services currently, in many cases schools are not resourced to provide children of deployed parents as much academic support as they need. The Army has also begun implementation of Student Online Achievement Resources (SOAR), an Internet-based application that provides tutorial lessons for children based on an assessment tool and resources for parents.

Programs designed to provide educational continuity to migrant children may provide additional insight into methods to support distance learning when necessary. Project SMART (Summer Migrants Access Resources through Technology), for example, broadcasts education programs for children, pairing a television teacher with a local teacher/facilitator who provides direct instruction and assessment, and offers students opportunities to keep up with their studies as they travel between states (Branz-Spall, Rosenthal, and Wright, 2003). Project ESTRELLA (Encourage Students through Technology to Reach High Expectations in Learning, Lifeskills, and Achievement) provides laptop computers to migrant students so that they can do schoolwork from any location; parents are also able to learn computer skills and help their children with school-work (Branz-Spall, Rosenthal, and Wright, 2003). Neither project has been evaluated, but could perhaps be adapted for military children's short-term separations from school.

Recommendation 5.1.2: Develop a set of procedures for schools to use in seeking Army Community Services (ACS) support to engage unresponsive parents.

Teachers reported that in rare cases, parents of children for whom deployment is particularly challenging were unresponsive and avoided contact with school staff. School staff discussed the need and desire in these rare cases to involve the military, but they were reluctant to do so for fear of getting the family in trouble. While schools that did have strong connections with the installation would ask for help in some cases, the process was described as largely informal, and staff requested a more formalized set of decision rules and processes by which schools could and should involve the Army. The Army Community Services could be engaged in these cases, but the school staff we interviewed were not aware of this resource. A set of procedures could be jointly developed by parents, school and military leaders, and School Liaison Officers for engaging ACS in difficult cases, and could be provided to school staff and military families at the start of the school year. One potential model may be Fort Riley and many of the schools in Geary County, which have developed a set of procedures that might serve as the basis for other schools and installations or for a more general Army-wide protocol.

Recommendation 5.1.3: Consider increasing transportation services for youth, particularly to facilitate their participation in after-school activities.

The interviews identified that transportation was a challenge for military children, who often were unable to participate in after-school activities because of the lack of transportation. While state and local dollars often fund support for transportation services during regular school hours, the installation may be able to offer support for one activity bus that could transport youth from school to the homes on post later in the afternoon, for example.

Currently, the Army is piloting a transportation program that would benefit from ongoing evaluation. Under the Army Family Covenant, 199 buses have been purchased for areas that have been highly impacted by deployment (e.g., Fort Carson, Joint Base Lewis-McChord). A number of installations provide bus transportation for off-post families to on-post after-school care and other resources. If the current program shows success, it could be expanded in more communities. Another cost-effective model may be to purchase a late bus route and/or additional bus stops, which would require some resources to pay for the driver and mileage, for example, but would not require the purchase of additional buses.

Recommendation 5.1.4: Advocate for full adoption and prompt, effective implementation of the Interstate Compact on Educational Opportunity for Military Children.

Some of the challenges that school staff discussed are ones that stem from the high mobility of the military population, which can be heightened during deployment. While children of military parents have traditionally been highly mobile due to parental change of assignment and/or location, parental deployments have compounded this problem as some parents move back home with their children to be closer to family and friends who may be able to provide additional support during the deployment.

In 2006, DoD began working on the Interstate Compact on Educational Opportunity for Military Children with the Council of State Governments. The compact sets timelines for academic record transfers, it requires new schools to honor class placements (e.g., Honors classes) and provide special education services comparable to what the student was previously receiving, and it provides additional excused absences just before deployment and during R&R and return times. The compact also allows students to waive state-specific courses and exams, provided they have completed a comparable course or exam in their previous state, and it requires states to create a council comprised of both education and military personnel, including a state military liaison responsible for helping military families and the state enact the compact's goals. Currently, 35 states have approved the compact, representing approximately 86 percent of military school-age children; 10 additional states are debating bills to approve the compact.[2]

The Interstate Compact on Educational Opportunity for Military Children, if implemented nationally (i.e., in all states), will help to address many challenges faced by children such as losing course credits and being required to meet new state requirements, or for children

---

[2] At the time of our interviews, only 11 states had enacted the compact. For more information, see National Center for Interstate Compacts (2010).

with special needs to be identified as such in the new state. Harmonizing state standards or transferability of state test scores, individual steps included within the compact, is also useful to pursue on a parallel track as states consider the broader compact.

However, even among states that have approved the compact, for some implementation has been slow. Therefore, monitoring and advocacy for the compact must continue even after state adoption. In addition, higher-level educational leaders, such as those in the U.S. Department of Education or in state and local education agencies, should be engaged to assess ways in which children of deployed military personnel can be more readily welcomed and integrated as full members of the local school community.

In addition to activities related to the Interstate Compact, the Army may also consider working with the Department of Education to develop a crosswalk or mapping of state standards by grade level. Every state has curriculum standards for kindergarten through grade 8. A resource that can help schools and parents compare the standards across all states would be useful in anticipating and addressing instructional gaps that will likely exist with a cross-state move. A resource like this may complement existing activities and tools provided by organizations such as the Military Child Education Coalition and the Military Impacted Schools Association.

Recommendation 5.1.5: Develop methods to inform schools about which children are military and the timing of parental deployments.

One of the major challenges cited by school personnel in our sample is that they often do not know who among their students have military parents; who have parents currently deployed; who are preparing for a parental deployment; and who are experiencing parental redeployment. School staff reported the need for better information so that appropriate services, supports, and accommodations may be put in place. This issue is particularly salient for children of Reserve and National Guard soldiers. Although such confidential information may raise initial concerns around security, schools are regularly privy to confidential information of their students and families in order to best support the child's educational needs and goals.

Teachers and counselors noted that more information about the status of military children may be gleaned by the schools themselves. At the beginning of the year, parents typically fill out information forms about the child. Schools might also ask at this time whether a parent is in the military, and if there are expected deployments or redeployments over the course of the school year, explaining the intention in asking such a question (response would be voluntary). Children and parents identified in this way could be informed of the various services that the school and Army provide to support them both in general and during the various phases of deployment. This would help provide schools with information about at least some of these children at a relatively low cost.

Ideally, and perhaps over the longer term (and at greater cost), the Army may consider ways to share sensitive information about parental deployment with schools. Three potential models are listed below which may help to inform the development of such a data sharing resource.

Foster Care. Potentially useful models for sharing sensitive information across agencies come from the foster care system. New York City is currently tracking children in the welfare system by an interdepartmental data-sharing agreement, and it maintains a database of school information for children in foster care (Conger and Finkelstein, 2003). Through this kind of information sharing, schools might also be able to access information about the child and family. Washington state has also developed a database (the Core Student Record System) that includes electronically updated information related to a student's education for all foster children. While also not yet formally evaluated, it is expected that this system will expedite the transfer of school records as students move (Conger and Finkelstein, 2003).

Highly Mobile Student Models. The New Generation System (NGS) is a web-based interstate information network that allows educators across the United States to record the progress of migrant students through the educational process. NGS captures educational and health data on migrant students if their state, region, or campus is a member of the NGS consortium, and teachers and schools may update the children's information upon school enrollment. This model, while not formally evaluated, might also be adapted to improve the transfer of information across states for military children when they move as well.

Immunization Registries. Most states maintain immunization registries to track the immunizations of children. Children are often required to have had certain immunizations before they are allowed to attend public or private schools, unless a waiver is granted. A limited number of immunization registries, including one in Washington, D.C., have formed unique partnerships with schools, whereby schools populate the immunization registries with current school enrollment data. Such data sharing allows for more targeted efforts by departments of public health and schools to improve immunization coverage rates, as well as helping school districts track immunization coverage in their schools. This model of information sharing between public health departments and schools might be adapted for information sharing between the Army and schools about deployments. While practical complexities surrounding confidentiality must be addressed, they are not insurmountable.

Recommendation 5.1.6: Expand efforts to educate school staff members, including classroom teachers, school nurses, and counselors, about the military.

Many of the school staff members that we interviewed expressed a need for understanding more about military life and what their students may be experiencing as a result of deployment. The DoD and DoE Memorandum of Understanding, signed in 2008 to improve the quality of education and address unique challenges faced by children of military families, called for the two departments to collectively "raise awareness among educators and community leaders about the impact of deployment and transfers on student achievement" (Department of Defense and Department of Education, 2008). Additionally, they will work together "on professional development opportunities to increase awareness of student transition and deployment issues related to the military students."

The military-school partnership could benefit from expanded use of training materials and courses to address gap areas articulated by school staff. Some efforts are already under way. For example, the Army is currently supporting the development of training programs by Military Child Education Coalition, Operation Military Kids and other organizations, and SLOs, in consultation with School Behavioral Health (SBH) staff, to organize support and educational workshops in some locations. Despite these efforts, the need for training among school staff persists. Further, school staff with whom we spoke shared challenges in translating training information into actionable strategies in the school setting. Potential training modules the Army might include:

- How to navigate and access military support services for children and families.
- How to interact with and assist students of military parents, both individually and in group settings, to address concerns about parent safety, health, and family stability.
- An overview of special issues facing elementary, middle, and high school age students that takes into account social and emotional developmental stages of these populations.
- An overview of special issues for students of Reserve and National Guard families.
- How to interact with and assist the nondeployed parent, particularly those parents with psychological or behavioral problems.
- How to address challenges and issues specific to the deployment cycle, including predeployment, deployment, block leave, and reunion.

One challenge voiced often by school staff was that training opportunities in their experience tend to include counselors and ancillary staff, but it is difficult for teachers to participate. School districts and DoD should jointly consider options for freeing up a selected group of teachers to participate in training (by, for example, funding substitute time), and then engaging these teachers to share this information with their fellow teachers post-training using a train-the-trainer model, for example. This may present an additional cost, but would allow teachers to participate in such training who have more interaction with students and play an important role in the identification of students who are struggling.[3]

Recommendation 5.1.7: Provide school counselors a way to easily and effectively access information on military support and services available to their families in need and increase awareness of this resource.

The school counselors we interviewed noted that they have limited information about how to help children and families link up with military resources, which contributes to their own feelings of frustration and stress. Even many of those who knew to look for specific websites found them difficult to use and were frustrated that no one single source could answer their disparate questions. For example, Military OneSource, a website that provides information on resources and support for military members, families, and providers, does not currently include a portal for school staff.[4]

One recommendation offered by several counselors was to have the military installation provide school counselors with a regularly updated resource guide, available on the Internet. A related suggestion, although one that would likely require greater resources, was to have a hotline to call for answers to questions on a variety of topics or for a name and direct number for the person who can help with specific problems. School counselors felt this would expedite receipt of services, and would be significantly less dependent on nonmilitary counselors trying to navigate the military system to acquire needed information.

---

[3] In schools that include a School Behavioral Health Program, the Army works with the schools to frame their relationship and expectations for cooperation, provides training for teachers and parents on issues concerning deployment and other topics, and has developed "train the trainer" models.

[4] The Army is currently developing a website to serve as a central resource for military school-related information for parents, teachers, counselors, and providers. The website is expected to have secure links for teachers and parents to fill out evaluation forms on children and adolescents who are being referred for care and follow-up. For schools supported by the School Behavioral Health Program, a hotline is provided with a single person who serves as the point of contact for each school.

The aim of the resource guide is to increase connections between individuals and information or services. For example, the Montana National Guard is in the process of designing a comprehensive resource guide for families before deployment, and a brief resource guide with contact information for each service to be distributed to families via their newsletter. A resource guide could be provided to local schools in areas where they are already in existence, while other areas may consider developing similar guides for their Reserve and Guard families, and sharing them with local schools as well.

Another option, which may have more far-reaching implications, would be to establish a mechanism for local Family Readiness Groups (FRGs) to connect with schools. Not only could FRGs provide school staff information on military resources, but they also are likely to have information on upcoming unit deployments and redeployments that can be shared with schools on a more informal basis.

Recommendation 5.1.8: Improve the presence of the School Liaison Officer (SLO) and enhance collaboration between SLOs and schools.

School staff we interviewed felt that with the current deployments, the SLOs were overburdened and were forced to prioritize their time and efforts on other issues. As a result, many schools reported that they are not receiving the necessary support and services from the military. The military may wish to consider expanding the number of SLOs, so that each serves only a limited number of school districts.

In addition to expanding the number of SLOs, our interviews revealed that there is essentially no SLO equivalent for the USAR or ARNG (technically the Reserve counterpart to the SLO is the School Transition Specialist, but these individuals serve many states at a time and are not known by school staff as a resource). This is likely because the School Support Program, which includes the SLOs, was originally designed to address the needs of military children who move frequently. As the SLO responsibilities have broadened to cover other aspects of military life including deployment, the SLO function is now more relevant to Reserve and Guard families. Given the unique challenges facing children of Reserve and Guard parents, the School Support Program should potentially be expanded to include these components.[5]

Because there appears to be no systematic process of accountability for the SLO, there is not a set of process and outcome metrics against which SLO accomplishments can be measured.[6] Considering the development of such a process of accountability may serve multiple functions. First, given that the SLO has numerous responsibilities that have likely changed over time due to the current conflicts, it may provide an opportunity for the Army to reevaluate where the SLO priorities should lie and how they should ideally spend their time. In the event that direct support to individual schools is no longer feasible (or desirable), other positions within the SLO office may be created to address current need. Second, it could provide important feedback to the Army about the effectiveness of the School Support Program. Receiving annual feedback from the schools may allow the Army to know where the SLO program is operating as intended, and to identify areas where additional supports or staff may be needed. Third, it might help create an important connection between the military and the schools.[7]

Recommendation 5.1.9: Revitalize the "Adopt-A-School" program.

Revitalizing the "Adopt-A-School" program might not only facilitate greater understanding of military culture and promote these connections, but the additional presence of service members in the schools may raise visibility and the need to share information about the installation and upcoming deployment schedules. The costs associated with this are primarily the cost of the soldiers' time, i.e., what is not getting done because the soldiers are at the school. As discussed above, however, frequent and large-scale deployments have made it challenging to

---

[5]   Since our research was conducted, the Army has expanded the School Support Program to the Reserve Components and added Reserve SLOs.

[6]   Since our interviews were conducted, the Army has developed a School Support Strategic Plan, which includes process outcomes and metrics and defines the role of the SLO, but not a universal set of performance measures for individual SLOs.

[7]   Since 2008, an additional 41 SLOs have been added, for a total of 141 Garrison SLOs.

sustain the program. Examining lessons learned from schools that have sustained their program over time may help to revitalize and maintain Adopt-A-School. As mentioned above in Recommendation 5.1.7, the "Adopt-A-School" concept may also be extended to Family Readiness Groups, which may be able to provide schools with a different set of resources and supports while further promoting connections between schools and the military.

Another potential model to build relationships between schools and Army installations comes from the U.S. Department of Agriculture (USDA). The USDA encourages field offices to adopt nearby schools, and it has created a guidebook for establishing Adopt-A-School relationships. The guidebook provides suggestions for partnership formats (e.g., instructional support, career guidance), steps for establishing a partnership, descriptions of the roles of agency coordinator and school contact, ideas for maintaining partnerships, and sample documents.[8] Although this guidebook has not been formally evaluated, it might provide useful suggestions.

5.2. Recommendations to Address Behavioral Health Needs of Children of Deployed Parents

One of the concerns raised by school staff and behavioral health providers was the limited number of child and adolescent specialists to serve military youth. Availability of TRICARE providers may be even lower in certain locations, particularly remote locations and further from military bases. It should be acknowledged that there is a national shortage of psychological and behavioral health providers, and specifically those with skills in addressing the needs of children and adolescents (Thomas and Holzer, 2006). Estimates of child psychiatrists per 100,000 youth also show the poor distribution of these providers, ranging from 1.3 in West Virginia to 17.5 in Massachusetts (Kim, 2003). A variety of other specialists are licensed to provide psychotherapy (psychologists, clinical social workers, counselors), but they often

---

[8]   For more information, see U.S. Department of Agriculture (1999).

lack specialty training in child psychological and behavioral health and are also disproportionately concentrated in urban areas (Thomas and Holzer, 1999).

While there is a well-documented shortage nationally, there are even fewer specialists who also have a background in military culture and the stressors of parental deployment (IOM, 2010, p. 5). Moreover, while there are some communities in which TRICARE provider networks have greatly enhanced services for children and adolescents, the availability of providers is still not geographically well distributed.

In addition to increasing the number of military counselors, it is also critical to consider the content of training offered to current providers, particularly as it relates to military culture and the potential stressors of deployment.

Recommendation 5.2.1: Continue to build psychological and behavioral health service capacity by increasing the number of military counselors.

As described above, many behavioral health experts and key stakeholders reported limitations in the availability of psychological and behavioral health services, particularly pediatric health providers.

Several initiatives and funding streams have been established to help address this area of need. For example, the FY2010 Defense Authorization included funds to strengthen DoD efforts to expand mental health care by increasing the number of military mental health providers and providing DoD scholarships to students pursuing mental health-related degrees. And effective July 1, 2008, students pursuing advanced degrees in mental and physical health fields are eligible for additional benefits upon joining the Army Medical Corps. The benefits cover all tuition and school-related costs, a stipend of more than $1,900 a month, and a $20,000 signing bonus for students agreeing to an eight-year commitment to the military (four years Active Duty, four years Reserve service obligation). The Army is also actively supporting and collaborating with schools to incorporate issues specific to the military in their curricula. For example, the University of South Carolina's Department of Social Work is offering degrees in Military

Social Work. Continuing to support these and similar programs may be important for ensuring a supply of trained providers.

The Army should also explore incentives and other benefits that might be offered to soldiers getting out of the Army who are interested in pursuing advanced degrees in related fields of psychology, marriage and family therapy (MFT), or peer counseling certifications. Troops to Teachers, a program that offers placement assistance and a stipend for teachers who work in an area of need, is a model that could serve as a useful guide for these efforts. Such a program could be facilitated through the Transition Assistance Program.

Recommendation 5.2.2: Continue to develop and implement provider training on military culture and potential impact of deployment.

Providers shared that they would benefit from more understanding of how deployment and reintegration affects each family member, the culture of the military installation, and what services (military and nonmilitary) may be available for their clients. Provider training for civilians from the Center for Deployment Psychology and the RESPECT-Mil Program (Re-Engineering Systems of Primary Care Treatment in the Military) (www.pdhealth.mil/respect-mil/index.asp) is designed to enhance provider capacity to understand military culture and to meet the unique service needs of soldiers with behavioral health needs. RESPECT-Mil is currently creating a module specific to the needs of youth and includes training for behavioral health providers as well as primary care providers and care facilitators.

Such provider training should continue to be developed and more widely implemented. For youth, provider training should be made available to not only behavioral health specialists but also those who traditionally address other health needs and may be important points of referral or screening for behavioral health issues, such as pediatricians and school nurses.

A broader dissemination of such provider training would also benefit those who offer free community-based behavioral health services to military families. There are a number of volunteer organizations that connect military families seeking services with behavioral health specialists, often for a prespecified number of visits. These providers may help families overcome barriers in accessing services such as stigma and appointment logistics by providing a nonmilitary, community-based resource. These providers, however, may not be as familiar with issues related to the military. This training could assist in enhancing the quality of these services and the use of practice that is evidence based with the military population.

Recommendation 5.2.3: Continue to expand models that support the prevention and treatment of behavioral health among hard-to-reach or remote youth populations.

Prevention. Promoting social networks among Reserve Component families could foster relationships among children, minimize feelings of isolation, and strengthen the general sense of community for Reserve and National Guard families. The Army should capitalize on and build upon existing family training and social events organized at either a regional or state level. For example, "Yellow Ribbon" events which take place before deployment, during deployment, and 30, 60, and 90 days post deployment are designed to share information and resources with families of Reserve and Guard soldiers.[9] Expanding youth programming at and around these events could provide an opportunity for networking, for sharing of resources among children experiencing various stages and lengths of parental deployment, and for helping to normalize their feelings and experiences.

Operation Purple Camp, free summer camps for children of military service members conducted through the National Military Family Association, is another opportunity to support the psychological and behavioral health of children. Among its goals, the camp aims to provide an opportunity for youth to connect with other children in the military and discuss the stress of parental deployment. A study of this program indicated that parents and children both felt that the camp was beneficial, and many planned to attend again in the future (Chan-

---

[9] The Yellow Ribbon Reintegration Program, established in 2008 for USAR and ARNG members and their families, includes Joint Family Resource Centers that organize resources for every state including deployment support and reintegration programs to provide information, services, referrals, and outreach opportunities.

dra et al., 2008). Operation Military Kids (OMK) also offers summer camps for military children, although they have not been formally evaluated, and vary by state. Camps or events specific to the USAR or ARNG could be organized through OMK, with the help of OMK's community partners. Expansion of either of these camps could provide a useful venue for convening children of Reserve and National Guard soldiers.

To support the continuation and maintenance of friendships established at regional events or summer camps, and to foster the development of new ones, the USAR and ARNG could design a social networking website for children to connect with their peers. While social networking activities are likely occurring informally among youth already, this approach would allow for greater parental control and closer monitoring of content. The site could host instant messaging, chat rooms, message boards, and blogging. This site could also provide links to resources/services available to Reserve Component families.

Treatment. Discussions with military behavioral health providers suggested that the use of telepsychiatry was increasingly being used for those youth who were far from a military hospital or unable to access local behavioral health services. Telepsychiatry is particularly critical for Guard and Reserve youth, who may not live near a military installation, but may benefit from a provider who understands military culture. At the time of data collection, Fort Bragg and Fort Drum were using this approach to extend their reach to youth and families.

The use of telepsychiatry has greatly expanded since our initial data collection. For example, Telepsychiatry and Community Mental Health Service's mission is to expand the availability of mental health assets to outlying military treatment facilities (MTFs) that have limited mental health resources by using the technological advances of interactive video and a number of programs to support psychological health of children and families; the MTFs are starting to include telehealth capabilities as part of their services.

In the civilian sector, telepsychiatry programs have shown positive results for pediatric populations (Nelson, Barnard, and Cain, 2003; Pignatiello et al., 2008). Meta-analysis has also found that while more long-term study is required, videoconferencing appears to be both feasible and effective (García-Lizana and Muñoz-Mayorga, 2010). Parents and youth also reported high satisfaction with telepsychiatry services, though this satisfaction was greater among parents of elementary school children than parents of adolescents (Myers, Valentine, and Melzer, 2008).

Recommendation 5.2.4: Enhance integration of behavioral health services with primary care, particularly in those clinics and hospitals serving military populations.

Another recommendation raised by behavioral health providers was better integration of behavioral health screening and services in more traditional primary care settings. While the integration of these services has become more common in nonmilitary settings, many of the providers serving military families felt that the potential of these models had not been fully realized for their clients. Since the time of data collection, the RESPECT-Mil program has greatly expanded its efforts to create a system of primary care to enhance the recognition and high-quality management of Post-Traumatic Stress Disorder (PTSD) and depression. RESPECT-Mil includes a treatment model designed by DoD's Deployment Health Clinical Center (DHCC) to screen, assess, and treat Active-Duty soldiers with depression and/or PTSD. RESPECT-Mil uses the Three Component Model (3CM) of care, featuring the coordination of primary care providers, care facilitators, and behavioral health specialists in the unique service of soldiers with behavioral health needs (see www.pdhealth.mil/respect-mil/index.asp). The Army is also developing Child and Family Assistance Centers (a pilot program at the Madigan Army Medical Center is currently in place), which is expected to include training of primary care managers and, with the Mayo Clinic and Columbia University, developing a three-day training seminar for primary care managers. The first training session is expected to take place at JBLM in the spring of 2011.

Further work in this area may draw upon civilian sectors, where pediatricians are increasingly identifying and treating psychological and behavioral disorders, including depression, among their patients (Kelleher et al., 1997; Horwitz et al., 1992; Glied and Cuellar, 2003).

Further, primary care providers are exploring alternative technologies to facilitate screening. For example, Chisolm and colleagues (2007) examined the feasibility of using the e-Touch system, a laptop approach to querying teens about depression, substance use, and risk of injury. They found that teens were satisfied with this approach if they felt that the system was easy to use. The screen used well-validated measures of risk, including items from the Youth Risk Behavior Survey (YRBS) and the Comprehensive Addiction Severity Index for Adolescents (CASI-A) of the Centers for Epidemiologic Studies Depression Scale for Children (CES-DC). While many providers cite issues of referral given the lack of specialty psychological and behavioral health services, a study by Richardson et al. (2007) found that most practitioners felt obligated to treat depression in their patients or at least to provide a stopgap until a referral could be secured.

Recommendation 5.2.5: Increase access to psychological and behavioral health services by augmenting school health services.

A recent IOM (2010) report identified an increase in mental or behavioral health diagnoses among military youth (p. 79), suggesting that efforts that may be able to identify or prevent these problems early are merited. Prevention programs, screening, and early intervention for behavioral health problems can reduce the need for more intensive and subsequent behavioral health services if left untreated. Although prevention, screening, and early intervention services are offered in some schools and in some primary care settings, there is much room for improvement.

Many of the respondents in this study perceived that limited access to services and stigma surrounding services made it difficult for students and families to obtain needed care. There is often a stigma associated with seeking psychological and behavioral care, and research provides evidence of this stigma for military service members (Hoge et al., 2004; OIF/MHAT, 2003; OIF-II/MHAT-II, 2005; MHAT-III, 2006a; MHAT-IV, 2006b). Addressing these potential barriers is important.

School psychological and behavioral health services may be able to overcome some of these challenges of location and stigma. Further, psychological and behavioral health services that are offered in schools have been linked to greater improvements in functioning compared to students served in a local clinic (Armbruster and Lichtman, 1999). Some states (North Carolina, Texas) are beginning to offer family counseling as part of their school psychological and behavioral health care. For both children and home caregivers, increasing the availability of counseling during and after school hours may assist in addressing the stress, depression, and related difficulties from a deployment or parental reintegration. Further, since there are very few psychological and behavioral health services designed specifically for the military child, developing treatment models for this population in school could be very useful.

Recommendation 5.2.6: Improve family engagement in behavioral health services.

Another issue that emerged in the interviews with providers was how to initiate and maintain engagement in behavioral health services. Recruitment and retention of families in child psychological and behavioral health services is difficult across populations in general, but for military families, issues of time, stigma, and other factors may make it particularly challenging. Work by McKay and Hibbert et al. (2004) may be useful in enhancing engagement in psychological and behavioral health services. An analysis of their engagement intervention, which includes telephone engagement early in the treatment process, has shown improvements in "show rates" between the first and second patient visit. The intervention includes a conversation with the parent or primary caregiver to clarify the need for child psychological or behavioral health services, to maximize a sense of efficacy in help-seeking, and develop strategies to overcome attitudinal and logistical barriers. Other researchers have also identified the benefits of telephone-based, family engagement strategies to encourage continuity of care (Szapocznik, 1988). Further, there is a wealth of research on brief motivational interventions (BMIs) to help clients prepare for treatment initiation and to maintain engagement in treatment (Moyers and Rollnick, 2006).

Recommendation 5.2.7: Provide school counselors and school nurses with up-to-date information on military and community psychological and behavioral health services.

Given the psychological and behavioral health issues faced by some students and parents, school leaders requested that more effort be placed on providing linkage assistance for obtaining psychological and behavioral health services.

While school counselors primarily have academic functions, many of the counselors we interviewed were providing some support for military youth via short, one-on-one counseling and deployment support groups. However, they reported that they were limited in their ability to provide to families referral names or resource lists of available psychological and behavioral health services on base or in the community. While these counselors cannot directly refer a child, providing schools with current information about available services and providers may assist in improving linkages to timely and appropriate care. In addition, school nurses may be viewed as a referral contact for youth who may visit the nurse for other health issues. Although the Office of the Secretary of Defense, Military Community and Family Policy is in the process of creating such a resource list for schools, installation-level resources and points of contact may be particularly helpful.[10] Many of the recommendations above in section 5.1, which seek to improve communication between schools and the military, could be expanded at little cost to address issues related to psychological and behavioral health services as well.

Recommendation 5.2.8: Improve evaluation of the MFLC program by integrating some outcomes-based measurement.

MFLCs provide necessary student family and staff support in schools. However, no individual client records are kept, making it challenging to assess the quality and effectiveness of the program in serving family needs. At the very least, some aggregate counts derived

---

[10] As stated above, the Army is developing a website to serve as a centralized resource that is expected to include secure links for teachers and parents to fill out evaluation forms on children and adolescents who are being referred for care and follow-up.

from process and outcomes-based metrics could be useful. The addition of a limited number of measures could capture valuable information and should not unnecessarily burden MFLCs, as such assessments can build upon information that is currently being collected but not formally documented. These measures could shed some light on the program:

- Number of referred unique youth/families who connect with community-based follow-up services.
- Number or percentage of unique youth/families who are satisfied with MFLC services, based on an anonymous survey, for example; such a survey could also capture the percentage who report improvements in symptoms, stressors, and/or challenges.
- Percentage of unique school staff who are knowledgeable about MFLC presence and availability of MFLC for students/families.
- Number of times (or relative percentage) MFLC uses evidence-based practice with students.

5.3. Future Directions

While this study advances the field with respect to understanding the perspectives from teachers and counselors about how military youth are coping with deployment and the issues that they confront in the school setting, it also identifies additional research questions in the areas of academic and behavioral health needs.

Recommendation 5.3.1: Monitor the impact that deployment is having on children in an academic setting over time.

To understand whether the negative association between parental deployment and academic achievement may be causally linked and whether the relationship persists, the Army should examine longitudinally the academic performance of children of soldiers. Our analysis included children from 2002 to 2008, and could only track students as long as they remained in state. Studying the long-term impact of deployment on children even as they move across states would help the

Army understand whether adverse effects persist. Longitudinal analysis, which includes children of soldiers who have not deployed, would also enable the Army to explore the impact that higher concentrations of children of deployed soldiers is having on Army children as a whole. Studies in particular of elementary and middle school students might aid in the early identification of shifts in academic performance, which is crucial when children are learning basic reading and math skills, and in middle school, when the dropout rate begins to trend upward. Further, given the possible link between academic issues and the behavioral health needs of students, it will be critical to quantitatively identify if and where relationships exist between academic challenges and preceding, concurrent, or subsequent behavioral health issues. This type of analysis will offer insight into where intervention juncture points exist, particularly to identify and mitigate problems early.

Recommendation 5.3.2: Quantitatively assess effects of deployment associated with other academic performance measures.

Given our qualitative findings noting that according to the school staff we interviewed, at least for some children, there are academic challenges associated with parental deployment, it will be important to extend future analyses beyond annual test scores. There is a need to conduct analyses using additional metrics of academic success and school behavior that may be more sensitive to the rapid changes that deployment brings. Such analyses may also help to identify early indicators that may signal potential struggles with parental deployment. Such metrics might include academic engagement (e.g., attending to tasks in class, coming prepared to class), quarterly grade point average, school connectedness, disciplinary issues, extracurricular involvement, on-time high school or grade-level completion, and postsecondary activities including college and/or military service entrance.

Recommendation 5.3.3: Examine whether deployment is having an impact on symptoms or behavioral health diagnoses.

Although little empirical data has been collected to date to provide insight into how deployments affect children's behavioral health over time, research suggests that children and adolescents experiencing a current parental deployment demonstrate significantly more behavior problems and have poorer psychological health, on average, than the general child and adolescent population (Chartrand et al., 2008; Flake et al., 2009). Further, compared to historical military samples, rates of such psychosocial problems appear to have increased in recent years (Flake et al., 2009; IOM, 2010).

The qualitative research with front line responders including teachers, counselors, psychological and behavioral health providers, and other medical professionals also suggests that the added stress of parental deployment may lead to social/emotional and behavioral difficulties. Further, teachers and counselors reported their belief that many of the academic challenges faced by their students, including low rates of homework completion, increased school absenteeism, and drops in grades, were linked to underlying psychological and behavioral health issues associated with parental deployment.

While our findings suggest that parental deployment may negatively impact the psychological health of some children and youth, numerous research gaps remain. First, we were unable to quantify the degree to which each theme is impacting schools and military children and families. Next steps may include a more systematic survey to a larger number of school staff in multiple geographic locations to help the Army identify which of the identified issues are the most widespread. It is also not clear whether a possible increase in symptomatology translates into higher rates of diagnosable psychological and behavioral health disorders. Despite recent articles suggesting a post-deployment increase in mental health visits, those analyses only capture persons who successfully accessed services and may not represent the full spectrum of symptomatology and need (Gorman, Eide, and Hisle-Gorman, 2010). The distinction between symptomatology and diagnoses is an important one, as the programmatic and policy solutions to address each scenario vary significantly. If, for example, there has been an increase in specific psychological or behavioral health disorders such as major depressive disorder or generalized anxiety disorder, identifying solutions to increase access to child and adolescent behavioral health specialists may be warranted, particularly if the illness requires evidence-based medical intervention. On the other hand, if the increase in poorer psychological health observed by previous studies is due to an increase in symptomatology, but still at a level low enough not to meet clinical criteria for diagnosis, different strategies such as increasing wraparound services in the schools or community—such as support groups or individual therapy by counselors—may be more appropriate and cost-effective. It is also important to interpret any increases in light of potential changes in awareness of problems and reporting practices.

Recommendation 5.3.4: Examine trends in met and unmet psychological and behavioral health needs using claims data.

An important and, as of yet, mostly untapped resource for understanding the effect of parental deployment would be an analysis of claims data that links psychological and behavioral health service utilization with characteristics of parental deployment.[11] While such an analysis would shed light on the impact of parental deployment on psychological and behavioral health issues of children, it would not capture unmet need—those individuals who need services but are not seeing a provider. This is a critical issue; in the general population, 75 to 80 percent of children and youth in need of mental health services do not receive them (Kataoka, Zhang, and Wells, 2002). Even if the Army is performing better than its civilian counterparts in serving children and youth with psychological and behavioral health needs, there is a high likelihood that a significant proportion of dependents still have unmet needs. While we heard reports of long wait times to see providers and a lack of provider availability during the course of this study, particularly among pediatric psychiatrists, there is little empirical evidence quantifying the scope and extent of the problem. Given that this may be an important bottleneck in the military mental health system for children and youth in particular, it warrants closer examination.[12]

---

[11] Recently, Gorman, Eide, and Hisle-Gorman (2010) documented increases in insurance claims for behavioral health services.

[12] The Army is currently examining utilization rates and projected needs based on the literature and limited data on need from unpublished studies conducted at Tripler Army Medical Center.

A last issue that warrants further investigation is whether children are receiving recommended treatment protocols by appropriate personnel. No studies to date have examined whether children are seeing clinicians trained at a level that is appropriate for their current needs. For example, children with more mild psychological and behavioral health problems may be able to be treated by master's level clinicians in a way that is not only more cost-effective, but that frees up time for child psychiatrists and other Ph.D. level clinicians to manage children with more severe psychological and behavioral problems. It may be that a more effective screening and triage system could alleviate some of the burden of the current system while still appropriately serving the needs of children and youth. More generally, an evaluation of outcomes and use of evidence-based practices regardless of provider types is also warranted.

Recommendation 5.3.5: Identify a comparable civilian cohort to assess similarities and differences in behavioral health service use rates.

Given the hypothesis that parental deployment is related to an increase in psychological and behavioral health problems, it is reasonable to want to directly compare rates of disorders between military and civilian children and adolescents. This comparison, however, is challenging for several reasons.

First, unlike the military population, where there are centralized databases for the vast majority of health care claims and diagnoses, there is no parallel database in the civilian population. While data from specific clinical settings or insured groups are available, populations vary widely in important demographics such as age, gender, and socioeconomic status, which may affect the case mix and hence the reported prevalence of disorders in the clinical setting under study.

Second, while epidemiologic research provides population-level estimates in the community, the estimates vary widely, depending on the diagnostic method used, age of the study sample, and time frame. For example, studies have reported on the prevalence of a given disorder ranging from current prevalence (i.e., currently have the disorder) to lifetime prevalence (i.e., ever had the disorder); this makes direct comparisons across studies and with military claims data for a single calendar year difficult. Commonly cited estimates for the prevalence of child and adolescent mental disorders come from the National Institute of Mental Health Methodology for the Epidemiology of Mental Disorders in Children and Adolescents (MECA) study, conducted in 1991–1992. The MECA study found that about 13 percent of children and adolescents had anxiety disorders, 6.2 percent had mood disorders, 10.3 percent had disruptive disorders, and 2 percent had substance-use disorders. It is not clear, however, whether rates have changed over time as diagnostic criteria have changed and methods of assessing such disorders have become more precise.

Third, the criteria used to diagnose a child or adolescent with a psychological or behavioral health disorder may vary widely among military providers. Given that the vast majority of reporting providers are social workers, psychologists, and pediatricians, rather than child psychiatrists who may use more standardized assessment tools such as the Diagnostic Interview Schedule (DIS) to establish Diagnostic and Statistical Manual of Mental Disorders-IV (DSM-IV) criteria, there may be significant variability in reporting standards even within the Army data. Such variability may make comparisons with civilian data even more challenging.

Taken together, direct comparisons between rates of psychological or behavioral health disorders among military and civilian populations will require a study that could assess similar claims data, with a comparable population, during the same time period. Data do not currently exist to facilitate such a direct comparison.

Recommendation 5.3.6: Examine the alignment of current army and civilian programs with youth academic and behavioral health needs.

Based on this and other studies of youth from military families, there has been a stronger call for evaluation of the current programs that serve this population. It will also be important to examine whether and to what extent the actual content of existing Army and civilian programs is aligned with the academic and behavioral needs identified in our analysis. This study was not intended as a comprehensive program gap analysis whereby we inventory the landscape of programs serving Army youth and assess the match of these services to needs, including target subgroups by location, component, age, or gender. However, a study that explores this content consistency is needed to highlight where curriculum and training fits the types of needs school staff reported, including youth stress, parent engagement, and academic progress.

Military families deserve no less than the best services available to support them during their service to our country. This study is one of the first important steps toward learning more about the challenges providers and school staff perceive military children face when a parent deploys and how educators, school psychologists, social workers, nurses, and all health and human services providers can support their academic success, and their social and emotional well being in public elementary, middle, and high schools.

Resources Available to Support Army Families

This appendix offers a brief overview of some of the resources available to support Army Families.

Academic and Social Support

Military-sponsored, military-supported, and community-based services play a critical role in supporting families and children when a parent deploys. Most Army-sponsored programs fall under Child, Youth and School Services (CYSS), which falls under the Family and Morale, Welfare and Recreation Command. Included in CYSS are child development centers, which are on-post child care centers that offer full-day, part-day, and hourly care for children, with additional hours of care for children of deployed parents. CYSS also provides School Age Services and Youth Services such as before- and after-school programs, weekend activities, summer care, and camps. Army CYSS also oversees the School Support Program, which includes School Liaison Officers (SLOs). SLOs function as liaisons between schools and the Army, originally to help ease the transition between schools when a family relocates, but more recently also to help families and schools with deployment-related issues. SLOs also provide information and assistance to families and school officials as necessary, and work collaboratively with schools to improve education for military children.

CYSS also works in conjunction with community organizations such as 4-H and the Boys and Girls Clubs of America to maintain Operation Military Kids (OMK). OMK provides social and educational programs and encourages children to build social connections with other military children. The organization also offers training for educators and service providers who work with military families. OMK is organized at a state level, and states vary in the number and types of programs offered. Family Readiness Groups (FRGs) also provide informal support and can be a source of information about the resources available to military families.

Family services are also available to ARNG personnel and their families through the National Guard Family and Youth Program. These include FRGs, information and referrals to social services, after-school programs, and family social events. As with OMK, the National Guard Family and Youth Program is organized by state, and states vary in the types of programs they offer, as well as in the extensiveness of the services available. Many of the services provided are listed on the Army One Source (AOS) website, particularly those of Reserve soldiers who are geographically dispersed and therefore have less access to military installation services.

There are many organizations that are independent from the military but provide support to service members and their families directly or indirectly. For example, the National Military Family Association (NMFA) works to educate military families about the benefits and services available to them, and advocates for policies that support service members and their families. The Military Child Education Coalition (MCEC) promotes quality education for military children and provides training and support for educators, parents, and children.

Behavioral Health Support

Behavioral health support to families is provided primarily through TRICARE. Currently, TRICARE, the predominant insurer for Army children, covers a range of behavioral or psychological health services. Families can schedule an appointment with a network behavioral health specialist without a referral from their primary care manager (PCM). Families can access the first eight outpatient psychological and behavioral health visits per fiscal year (October 1–September 30). For any services after that eighth visit, prior authorization is required. However, if a family chooses to see a licensed professional counselor, that referral and care must be authorized by a physician regardless of whether the counselor is in the TRICARE network. Inpatient services require referral and prior authorization, consistent with other insurance plans.

Coverage for specific types of treatments varies. TRICARE covers a range of psychotherapy, acute inpatient psychiatric care, and partial hospitalizations for combinations of day, night, and weekend programs. Residential treatment centers provide extended care for children and adolescents (some up to age 21) who have psychological disorders that require continued treatment in a therapeutic environment. TRICARE covers 150 days in a TRICARE-authorized residential treatment center per fiscal year. TRICARE may cover more days if determined to be medically or psychologically necessary. However, residential treatment center care is not covered for emergencies. Further, admission primarily for substance-use rehabilitation is not authorized.

The Military Family Life Consultant (MFLC) program provides behavioral health support in schools. This program is broadly designed to provide support and assistance to soldiers in the Active and Reserve Components, military family members, and civilian personnel. MFLCs can serve as a much-needed resource to students, families, and school staff. For schools that have an MFLC assigned to them, many of the issues and concerns raised by staff are the focus of the MFLCs. MFLCs not only provide training and information to teachers, counselors, and administrative staff about military life, culture, and the impact that parental deployment may have on children, but they also can provide specific strategies to help teachers better support a struggling student in the classroom.

Although MFLCs are housed in schools, they are not considered school staff. The program was specifically designed in this way to enhance student and parent comfort and address issues of stigma. Services are confidential and anonymous and are not linked to either the military or the schools. For students and families, MFLCs provide nonmedical consultation, that is, they do not provide therapy or counseling; if therapy is needed, the student or family is referred out. MFLCs work with students on an individual basis to develop strategies and tools that the student can use to overcome his or her current challenges (e.g., high levels of stress, worry, sadness, anger). There are currently 158 MFLCs in schools across the country.

There are also national, state, and local efforts to increase military families' access to psychological and behavioral health care providers. For example, Military OneSource offers consultation, referrals to service providers, and free counseling sessions for soldiers and their families. Similarly, Give an Hour is a national organization offering free, confidential counseling services to military families. A number of regional, state, and local providers also offer free psychological and behavioral health care to service members and their families; they include Returning Veterans Resources Project in the Pacific Northwest, Strategic Outreach to Families of All Reservists (SOFAR) in New England, Support Our Family in Arms in Colorado, the Vermont Military, Family, and Community Network, and the Coming Home Project in the San Francisco Bay area.

We have discussed only a small fraction of the many programs created to serve families. A thorough discussion of the available programs is beyond the scope of this study, and new programs are added frequently. While these resources are helpful to many Army families, the availability and comprehensiveness of specific programs often vary by location and gaps remain. There has also been relatively little research to understand what gaps currently exist in support for families before, during, and after deployment; which programs are most effective; and how the programs might be improved to offer better support to a greater number of families. RAND is currently in the process of compiling a more comprehensive and extensive assessment of the programs that are available.

Methods

This appendix provides additional details on the methods for both the quantitative (Chapter Two) and qualitative (Chapters Three and Four) analyses.

Quantitative Methods

Sample

Our sample included 44,654 children or dependents of soldiers in the Regular Army (also referred to in this report as Active soldiers) who serve full-time in the Army, as well as U.S. Army Reserve and Army National Guard soldiers, who perform part-time duties except when mobilized. Children resided in North Carolina (31,535) or Washington (13,119) and attended public elementary, middle, or high schools. Dependents of Active-Duty, U.S. Army Reserve and Army National Guard soldiers from both the enlisted and officer corps are included in this analysis.[1]

Among children of Active soldiers, nearly two-thirds attend public schools both on-post and off-post (comparable data for children of Reserve and Guard soldiers is not available). See Table B.1.

---

[1] For this research, Reserve and National Guard soldiers who have been activated are considered part of the Reserve and National Guard forces to distinguish them from Regular Army soldiers who serve full-time.

Table B.1
School Attended by Children of Army
Active-Duty Soldiers, Grades K–12

School Type	%
Public school off-post	52
Public school on-post	12
Department of Defense school	20
Private school	8
Other	8

SOURCE: Defense Manpower Data Center,
Survey and Program Evaluation Division (2007).

Data

To examine the relationship between parental deployment and academic performance, we linked data by student from two sets of sources: (1) state education data on academic testing scores and student demographics and (2) Department of Defense and Army data on soldiers and deployment. From each state, we include scores from standardized tests. In North Carolina during the period under examination (2002–2007), elementary and middle school students took End-of-Grade (EOG) Reading and Math Tests each year, which are administered to most students in June. At the high school level, all students are also required to take an End-of-Course (EOC) Test in English I and Algebra I (although advanced students may take these courses and exams before high school). In Washington, students were administered the Washington Assessment of Student Learning (WASL), which consists of examinations over four subjects (reading, mathematics, science, and writing). It is given to students from third to tenth grade, though it is not required in the ninth grade. In each year during the 2002–2007 timeframe, reading and math are administered; science and writing are administered only in select grades.

Our analysis includes all dependents of soldiers who listed North Carolina or Washington as their permanent or temporary residence at some point during the period 2000–2007 in the Defense Enrollment Eligibility Reporting System (DEERS) and attend public school. DEERS maintains personnel and benefits information for Active, retired, and Reserve uniformed service personnel, eligible family members of Active, retired, and Reserve uniformed service personnel as well as DoD civil service personnel and some DoD contractors. Deployment data, obtained from DMDC's Contingency Tracking System, is captured as a monthly bivariate data element, which is equal to 1 if the soldier is deployed that month and 0 otherwise.[2] The number of months deployed at the time the test was administered was computed directly from the underlying data, using the 15th of the month as the day of deployment. The number of deployments was calculated as the number of uninterrupted spells deployed during a particular period, including spells that began before the start of the period and those that were still ongoing at the end. Where a soldier had a deployment of four or more months, followed by one month not deployed, and then a second deployment of four or more months, the month not deployed was considered to be leave from deployment and not an end of deployment.

Other data on soldiers was obtained from the Work Experience (WEX) File, Active Pay Files, Reserve Pay Files, the Total Army Personnel Database/Active Enlisted (TAPDB/AE), the Total Army Personnel Database/Active Officer (TAPDB/AO), and the Reserve Components Common Personnel Data System (RCCPDS).

The student-level covariates included in the model are age, gender, grade, socioeconomic status (as measured by whether the child is entitled to a free lunch, a reduced lunch, or neither), and the year of the test. The parent-level covariates are component (Active or Reserve/National Guard), whether the soldier is an officer or enlisted, seniority, years of service, race/ethnicity, education level (less than a high school degree or equivalent, high school degree or equivalent, and greater than high school degree or equivalent), age, and gender. Seniority is defined by three categories as follows: Junior = E1–E4 (Private to Specialist or

---

[2] The Contingency Tracking System (CTS) Deployment File includes all U.S. military personnel who have been deployed in support of the Global War on Terrorism, i.e., Operation Enduring Freedom (OEF) and Operation Iraqi Freedom (OIF) from September 11, 2001 to the present. It is updated monthly and includes a separate individual record for every deployment event, for each member. For the Army, deployment begins when a soldier is on the ground in an AOR and is therefore eligible for hostile fire pay. A soldier is entitled to a month of hostile fire pay if he or she spent any portion of that month in theater.

Corporal) for enlisted soldiers, O1–O3 (Second Lieutenant to Captain) for officers; Mid-Grade = E5–E6 (Sergeant to Staff Sergeant) for enlisted soldiers, O4 (Major) for officers; Senior = E7–E9 (Sergeant First Class to Sergeant Major) for enlisted soldiers, O5–O10 (Lieutenant Colonel to General) for officers. These values vary by year to account for promotions and change of status.

Analyses

To make the results comparable across grades, subjects, and year, original scaled test score results were normalized relative to statewide distributions in each grade and subject with a mean of 0 and a standard deviation of 1. Therefore scores are presented as normalized z-scores, with negative scores below the statewide average and positive scores above.

The primary model in our analysis is specified in Equation B.1. To examine the relationship between parental deployment and achievement, we use scaled scores in reading and math (and for North Carolina in high school English I and Algebra I) for individual students as the outcome of interest. Formally, the model is specified as:

$$Y_{ikt} = \mu_t + \alpha D_{it} + \beta X_{itk} + \gamma P_{it} + \delta_{kt} + \varepsilon_{ikt}, \qquad (\text{B.1})$$

where Y_{ikt} is the normalized scale score in reading, English I, math, or Algebra I for student i, attending school k, in year t. μ_t is the intercept at the time t of interest, D_{it} is a vector of indicators of parent deployment at time t, X_{itk} is a vector of student-level covariates, P_{it} is a vector of parent-level covariates, δ_{kt} are independent school (or, in some cases described below, student) random errors, and ε_{ikt} are independent student random errors. In the model the parameter α estimates the association of deployment and the performance score, β estimates the effect of student characteristics, and γ estimates the effect of parental characteristics.

Often in education analyses, researchers will perform a statistical adjustment to account for schoolwide variables. Each student in the sample is not an independent observation, but may attend the same school as another student in the sample. Schoolwide factors such as the quality of the teaching and classroom size may influence a student's academic testing score, so the test scores of the students in the sample too are not independent. To account for this, researchers will cluster-adjust the sample by school. However, this was not possible with the North Carolina sample, since many students changed schools during the period of analysis (2002–2007). As a result, estimation of the school effect (δ_{kt}), alongside other necessary covariates, was often not possible. When trying to estimate the models, we no longer had a nested structure, and the effect on each student's test score can be attributable to multiple schools. Understanding those various dimensions require a number of matrix inversions that could not be performed on these data. Therefore, the results we present here are cluster-adjusted by student (because a student may appear in our sample multiple times), but not by school. There were some models that could be fit even after cluster adjusting for school (for example when we evaluated the results by year or by grade). The results were consistent with those found when cluster-adjusting by student, so we do not believe that this alternative adjustment affected our conclusions.

Equation B.1 provides an overall estimate of the association between parental deployment and academic test scores, but we are also interested in understanding whether those relationships vary across a number of relevant factors (F). We examine whether the association between achievement and deployment varies by component, rank, seniority, and gender of the soldier, the grade and gender of the student, and whether these relationships are different in different years. The expanded model is displayed in equation B.2:

$$Y_{ikt} = \mu_t + \alpha_0 D_{it} + \alpha_1 F_{it} + \alpha_2 D_{it} F_{it} + \beta X_{itk} + \gamma P_{it} + \delta_{kt} + \varepsilon_{ikt}. \quad \text{(B.2)}$$

B.2. Qualitative Methods

Interviews with Experts and Key Stakeholders

Interviews were designed to elicit expert views on the academic and psychological and behavioral health challenges faced by children with deployed parents and their families, what programs and services are available to support these children, what characteristics of these programs or services are working effectively and what might be improved, and gaps in support for these children. Interviews with psychological and behavioral health care experts also included a discussion of the system of care available to dependents of Army soldiers in the Active and Reserve Components. Interviews were semi-structured and confidential. For the interview protocol, please see Appendix C. This protocol served as a guide but interviews were semi-structured and so each discussion may not have covered each topic, and may have included topics not contained in the protocols but relevant to that interview.

In total, the project team conducted 12 individual and group interviews with TRICARE leaders, clinical and pediatric behavioral health specialists,[3] and other key stakeholders including Military Family Life Consultants (MFLCs).

Interviews with Administrators, Teachers, and Counselors

We also conducted focus groups and interviews with school superintendents and principals and other administrators, teachers, counselors, and others involved with children of deployed soldiers to understand the challenges faced by children with deployed parents and their families; to identify issues that schools face while supporting these children; and to identify what programs and services are particularly beneficial or effective in promoting positive outcomes for children, issues that exist with current services that might be improved, and gaps where no programs and services are supporting a need that the Army should address in the future.

We conducted these focus groups and semi-structured interviews with teachers, counselors, and administrative staff (e.g., principals and vice principals) at twelve schools in the spring of 2008. Counselors included a range of staff from academic counselors to school social workers and psychologists. The twelve-school set was made up of one elementary school, one middle/junior high school and one high school

---

[3]   These interviews were with primarily TRICARE contract managers and providers. The providers were a mix of medical doctors, Ph.D.s, and licensed clinical social workers.

in each of four districts, two of which served the majority of families at one Army installation and two served the majority of families at another Army installation in a different region of the country. These installations were selected due to their continued and high rates of deployment. The two closest school districts to the post were selected for involvement in the study, and individual schools were identified by district-level staff or superintendents as having the highest proportion of military youth. Schools ranged in size from 588 students to 1,400 students. Three schools were situated on a Army post, where approximately 98 percent of the students were military youth. Estimates of the percentage of military children and youth attending schools not on post (the remaining nine schools) ranged from 30 percent to 70 percent, according to school personnel. It should be noted that schools generally do not have data on all families with a military parent, so percentages reported by schools are approximations. Staff reported on their perceptions of the current, previous (since 2001), and upcoming deployment experiences for both their current and former students.

At each school, approximately two administrative staff, three counselors, and six teachers participated in the study (N=132 staff). When possible, interviews and focus groups were held separately for administrators, counselors, and teachers. In addition, we conducted 16 phone interviews across the country with teachers, counselors, and administrative staff of public elementary, middle, and high schools serving Army Reserve or National Guard children, who may be more isolated and live further from a military installation. Staff was identified through snowball sampling, where those we interviewed recommended others whom we might interview of areas with high concentrations of Army Reserve and National Guard soldiers and through organizations that serve schools with Reserve and National Guard children.

Each focus group and interview began with a brief introduction of the study, and participants gave informed consent to participate. Focus groups lasted approximately one hour and were audio recorded. We asked school staff to comment on the following domains: (1) unique behavioral or emotional issues of children of military personnel, (2) unique social issues among children of deployed parents, and (3) unique academic issues faced by children of deployed soldiers. For each domain, we also sought to understand how these issues vary by age, gender, whether the parent is from the Active Component or Reserve or National Guard, length of deployment, and point in the deployment cycle (e.g., about to deploy, recently deployed, short periods home during block leave or R&R, recently returned home). For the interview protocol, please see Appendix C. As with the expert interview protocol, the school staff protocol served as a guide, but individual interviews may not have covered each topic, and may have included topics not contained in the protocols but relevant to that interview.

Our analyses were primarily qualitative. We first completed and edited all interview notes with the audio recordings and abstracted information on each study domain from supporting documents. We organized our data first by domain, further analyzing it by relevant themes. Three researchers reviewed the notes, separately abstracting themes, and then convened to discuss points of discordance.

Our findings presented in Chapter Three (on academic outcomes) and Chapter Four (on related psychological and behavioral health outcomes) do not reflect an exhaustive accounting of every issue raised by school staff, but rather highlight some of the major concerns and recommendations that emerged related to the academic and associated psychological and behavioral health needs of these children, particularly during deployment. Further, given the unique experiences of Reserve and Guard families, we highlight issues that are especially salient for these students.

There are a few caveats to these findings that are important to keep in mind. First, this research is based on the perspectives of those teachers, counselors, and school administrators who agreed to speak with us, and so the sample is a convenience sample. However, we obtained a diverse mix of school staff by grade and role to help minimize selection bias. Participant responses may also be biased by a lack of objectivity.

Second, our findings are based on interviews from school staff at two large installations and from staff working with Reserve and Guard children across the country. While general findings converged across locations, other communities may experience different challenges. Third, most of these interviews were conducted between March and

June 2008, and there may have been changes in perspective or in the availability of services since then as well as changes during the time period participants were recalling. Fourth, we did not attempt to validate these findings with objective data or attempt to assess the relative weight, severity, or prevalence of issues for military children compared with others. We do not believe, however, that any of these limitations to the research affect the nature of the conclusions or the relevance of the recommendations.

Interview Protocols

Explanation and Consent for Research Interview Participation

RAND, a nonprofit research institution, is studying how parental deployment affects school achievement and children's behavior in school. This study is sponsored by the Army. The goal of the study is to make recommendations on how the Army can improve its support of these students. We hope this will be an opportunity to provide input on strategies that may improve the services provided by the Army.

We are interested in talking with you to learn about issues that these students face in school. We also want to learn about programs or services offered in your school to help these students. Finally, we would like to hear about your ideas for how to improve those services. We selected your school because it has a large number of children whose parents are in the Army.

[FOR TEACHER/COUNSELOR GROUP INTERVIEW:]
[This will be a group interview. We will ask you some questions, and we will lead a discussion. But, this is your group. We want to hear what you have to say and we ask that you respect the opinions of others in the group.]

RAND will use the information you provide for research purposes only. Your responses will be kept confidential. We will not disclose your identity or information that would identify you to anyone outside of the project without your permission, except as required by law. Your responses will be combined with others and reported together. If quotations are used in any written reports, they will not be connected to an individual. At the end of the study, we will destroy any information that identifies you.

Taking part in this interview is voluntary. You may choose not to answer a question and you may [stop / leave] the interview at any time.

Do you have any questions before we begin? (If yes, ANSWER ANY REMAINING QUESTIONS)

The interview will take approximately [45 minutes / 1 hour].

- If you think of any questions after we leave [or have something you would like to say in private], please call Anita Chandra at 703.413.1100 x5323 (work). Dr. Chandra can also be reached by email at chandra@rand.org.

- Do you agree to participate in the interview?
  - If yes, continue with protocol.
  - If no: "That is fine. Thank you for your time." (LEAVE)

Whom to Contact About This Research:

Amy Richardson	Human Subjects Protection Committee
RAND	RAND Corp.
703-413-1100 x5145	310-393-0411, ext. 6369
amyr@rand.org	hspcadmin@rand.org

Effects of Multiple Deployments on Children's School Performance of Behavior

Interview

The goal of this project is to examine the impact that parental deployment has on the academic achievement and school behavior of children of Army soldiers, and to make recommendations on how the Army might improve its support of these children. As part of this work, we are conducting interviews at a number of school districts near select active or reserve component installations including yours. These interviews will help us identify challenges faced by children with deployed parents and their families; help to identify issues that schools face while supporting these children; and help to identify what programs and services are particularly beneficial or effective in promoting positive outcomes for children and families, and which could use improvement. Results of this work will inform our recommendations to the Army for how they may support the needs of these children more effectively in the future to promote positive academic outcomes.

[READ ORAL CONSENT]

Perspectives on Issues Facing Military Youth

[NOTE: THESE QUESTIONS MAY OVERLAP DEPENDING ON RESPONDENT ANSWERS, SO CAN SHORTEN AS NEEDED]

To start, we would like to hear a bit more about your experiences working with students who have families in the military, and your thoughts on the challenges, if any, that they face when a parent is deployed. Please think first about academic issues (e.g. test grades, homework completion, comprehension of new materials).

1. In your view, do these students face any unique academic issues in general? If so, what are these issues?

    a. Do you think these issues differ by the age of the student? [Probe: younger vs older students depending on school level]

    b. Do you think these issues differ for children of active duty vs. reserve or Guard personnel? Or the family's time in the military? [If school district is mostly active duty, query respondent on their ideas or perspectives on how it may differ]

    c. Do you see any changes in these issues over time? In other words, are there times when these issues are more pronounced, such as when a parent is deployed or comes home? If so, how?

    d. [for teachers/counselors] In your class [or with your students], how have you addressed these issues?

        i. Has anything been difficult about addressing these issues? If so, describe.

I would now like you to think about behavioral or emotional issues of these children (e.g. classroom behavior, suspensions, ability to remain focused on tasks).

2. In your view, do these students face any unique behavioral or emotional issues in general? If so, what are these issues?

    a. Do you think these issues differ by the age of the student? [Probe: younger vs older students depending on school level]

    b. Do you think these issues differ for children of active duty vs. reserve or Guard personnel? Or the family's time in the military? [If school district is mostly active duty, query respondent on their ideas or perspectives on how it may differ]

    c. Do you see any changes in these issues over time? In other words, are there times when these issues are more pronounced such as when a parent is deployed or comes home? If so, how?

      d. [for teachers/counselors] In your class [or with your students], how have you addressed these issues?
            i. Has anything been difficult about addressing these issues? If so, describe.

3. What about socially? Do these students face any unique issues? If so, what are these issues?
      a. Do you think these issues differ by the age of the student? [Probe: younger vs older students depending on school level]
      b. Do you think these issues differ for children of active duty vs. reserve or Guard personnel? Or the family's time in the military? [If school district is mostly active duty, query respondent on their ideas or perspectives on how it may differ]
      c. Do you see any changes in these issues over time? In other words, are there times when these issues are more pronounced such as when a parent is deployed or comes home? If so, how?
      d. [for teachers/counselors] In your class [or with your students], how have you addressed these issues?
            i. Has anything been difficult about addressing these issues? If so, describe.

[If not already raised in earlier sections]

Have you engaged other students in helping to address some of the issues that we discussed? If so, describe.

For counselors: Do you work with teachers to address any of the student issues that we have discussed? How do you work together?

For teacher: Do you work with your counseling staff to address any of the student issues that we have discussed? How do you work together?

Now that we have talked about the needs of students in military families, let's talk more about the programs available for these youth and where programs could be enhanced.

Information about Programs Offered [may overlap to Q1d, 2d, and 3d]

4. [Reference first section as appropriate] What programs or services, if any, do you currently offer students from military [Army] families? Please describe.
    a. Are these programs or services available to other non-military students? If no, were they newly created for these students? [Principal: Are they only available at this school or district wide?]
    b. [Principal: What motivated you to offer these programs or services for military students?]
    c. What has been the response of parents, and students (both military and non military) to these programs?
    d. How effective do you think they are?

5. In addition to the programs and services described earlier, do you connect students with any programs in the community? If so, what are they?
    a. What is the process of connecting students?
    b. What has been the response of parents, families to these programs?

We have just spent some time talking about the needs of children and the school services and programs available to them. I would now like you to think about some of the challenges and barriers to these programs as well as any critical gaps or needs that are not being addressed by currently available programs. In addition, we are very interested in your recommendations about how to overcome those gaps and address those barriers, what programs might need to be created, and anything else you would like to say about how to improve the outcomes for students.

Gaps in Programs or Services

6. What would you say are some of the challenges or gaps in providing effective services to these students?

[PROBE: Any others?]

[Probe in the following areas if not referenced:]

    a. Issues around school transitions
    b. Helping kids with academics, getting class or homework done
    c. Feeling connected at school (e.g., with other students, other military kids)
    d. Helping kids with coping, emotional health, stress
    e. Communication with parents/engaging parents
    f. Communication with and support from principal/school administrations
    g. Communication with Army—do they make you aware of time frame for deployments/redeployments so you have time to prepare [primarily for principal]
    h. Other?

7. What do you consider to be your biggest gap or challenge?

8. What do you think should or could be done to address it?

[PROBE: Anything else?]

[PROBE ON: the need for new or additional programs,
more support from the Army or broader community,
the need for additional resources.]

[Continue to probe until they say "no"]

> 9a–z. You also mentioned that [take from list above] was another {gap/challenge}. What do you think should be done to address that?

[PROBE: Anything else?]
[PROBE ON: the need for new or additional programs,
more support from the Army or broader community,
the need for additional resources.]

[Continue to probe until they say "no"]

[REPEAT #9 until all gaps/barriers have been discussed]

> 10. If you had a pot of resources (reasonable amount of money, other resources) to design a program for these children, what would that look like?

[PROBE ON: expected impact, any barriers to getting it up and running]

Army-Child Mental Health Project
Expert Interview Guide

Objectives of this research

- To describe the current system of care for child mental health within military health services, and barriers to service provision
- To describe other school-based and community-based mental health services available to these youth and gaps in services (to analyze variation by component (Active vs. Reserve/Guard) in terms of use and access)
- To outline a set of policy and programmatic options for addressing child mental health service issues, with attention to improving access and capacity in light of the need for cost-effective strategies

General questions

1. We are trying to get a sense of the need for child mental health services among youth from military families.
   a. Do you have an estimate of the prevalence of diagnosable mental or behavioral health problems (e.g., depression, anxiety disorder, ADHD) among the population you serve? Is this based on an analysis of your data (claims, etc) or a ballpark estimate?
   b. Have you seen an uptick of problems over the last few years, considering OIF/OEF deployments?
      i. If so, what kinds of problems do you (your providers) see at higher rates, or that you have never seen before?
      ii. Are there particular periods in deployment where you see an increase or a change? (R&R program helpful to the family?)

2. We hear about a lot of the barriers to obtaining mental health services for children from military families. What do you think

are the major challenges to service delivery for these children? [Probe on:]

    a. Access issues—payment, location of providers, transportation, etc

    b. Capacity—not enough providers, expertise or training of providers on military culture/deployment

    c. Attitudinal/perceptual—stigma, reluctance to seek care, or misperceptions about treatment benefit, quality, etc

    d. Referral process? (hard referrals, warm hand offs between PCPs and MH)

    e. Wait times?

    f. Other?

3. Some folks have talked about engaging non specialty MH providers, such as teachers, school counselors, etc, to address child mental health needs (even before it rises to a diagnosable condition), given the shortage in pediatric psychiatrists and psychologists. Have you tried these approaches in your organization? What do you think about this strategy?

4. [Other than anything described in #3] Are you (as provider/ health plan/program leader) or your organization doing anything different from usual practice to address child mental health issues for these youth from military families (particularly since the start of OIF/OEF)? If so, please describe.

5. As part of this analysis, we plan to visit a couple of installation communities to talk to military and community-based mental health providers, school leaders, and parents about accessing mental health services for youth. Do you have any suggestions for communities that you think:

    a. Have significant mental health need among their child population that they are working to address by increasing providers, trying creative strategies, etc?

      b. Are exemplar in how they are integrating military and community-based services

      c. Are addressing child mental health issues through school or community-based programs

6. As we move forward with this research, are there any particular questions regarding improving the system of care for military child mental health that you would like addressed, or answered? What do you think we are missing in the current discussion about policy and programmatic options?

Specific to health plans/insurers

1. [May have talked about claims data in general Q1] Have you done any analysis of your claims data for children who are being seen for mental health issues?

      a. If so, has this analysis informed your own cost analysis, capacity planning, etc?

      b. Is there unmet clinic need?

      c. Are you willing to share any data on prevalence, numbers of providers in your network?

2. Do you see geographic variation in child mental health needs among providers in your plan?

3. Where do you see gaps in TRICARE benefits for families?

Specific to providers

1. We hear a lot about wait times and not being able to accept new patients.

      a. Are you facing this challenge in your own practice?

      b. If so, how are you addressing this (probe on: referrals to other providers, providing pre-clinical or pre office-based services)

2. What supports do you need to better address the mental health needs of the children from military families that you see in your office/practice? (probe on: reimbursement issues, training, infrastructure such as EMR problems, other)

Specific to youth MH program leaders

1. Have you examined the effectiveness or impact of your program? If so, what have you found (get any data, reports if we can)
2. What challenges do you face to increase the reach of your program, particularly to children from Guard/Reserve families?
3. What kinds of supports do you need to sustain your program?

Model Results

In this appendix we provide a more detailed description of the regression results, including sample size, variable estimates, and robust standard errors.

Table D.1
The Relationship Between Deployment and Achievement Test Scores: Cumulative Months of Deployment Modeled Linearly

	Estimate (Robust Standard Error)					
	North Carolina				Washington	
	Reading	Math	English	Algebra	Reading	Math
Months deployed	−0.003**	−0.003**	−0.003*	−0.004*	−0.004**	−0.004**
	(0.001)	(0.001)	(0.002)	(0.002)	(0.001)	(0.001)
Component/rank						
Active-Duty officer	0.446**	0.428**	0.370**	0.285**	0.473**	0.549**
	(0.024)	(0.024)	(0.049)	(0.054)	(0.033)	(0.034)
Reserve/Guard enlisted	−0.007	0.046**	−0.031	0.005	−0.003	0.022
	(0.013)	(0.013)	(0.028)	(0.032)	(0.020)	(0.021)
Reserve/Guard officer	0.359**	0.437**	0.406**	0.240**	0.375**	0.475**
	(0.028)	(0.028)	(0.055)	(0.065)	(0.035)	(0.036)
Seniority						
Junior	−0.134**	−0.120**	−0.204**	−0.130**	−0.200**	−0.251**
	(0.015)	(0.014)	(0.041)	(0.046)	(0.028)	(0.028)
Mid-grade	−0.079**	−0.078**	−0.151**	−0.073**	−0.096**	−0.085**
	(0.010)	(0.009)	(0.023)	(0.026)	(0.018)	(0.019)
Years of service	0.001	0.002	−0.004	0.004	−0.001	−0.002
	(0.001)	(0.001)	(0.003)	(0.003)	(0.002)	(0.002)
N	49,554	49,982	6,847	4,762	12,902	12,960

NOTES: Also controlled for soldier race, education, age and gender, child age, gender and grade, socioeconomic status and year and cluster-adjusted for school (WA) and child (NC).

** statistically significant at 1 percent level.

* statistically significant at 5 percent level.

Junior = E1–E4/O1–O3; Mid-grade = E5–E6/O4; Senior = E7–E9/O5–O10.

Table D.2
The Relationship Between Deployment and Achievement Test Scores:
Cumulative Months of Deployment Modeled Linearly
(Calculations for Scale Scores)

	Estimate (Robust Standard Error)					
	North Carolina				Washington	
	Reading	Math	English	Algebra	Reading	Math
Scale score						
Mean	257.97	293.07	73.68	77.18	408.77	393.27
Standard deviation	9.16	42.68	34.99	33.79	24.6	38.62
Minimum	221	218	22	31	250	142
Maximum	289	386	176	181	541	619
Effect size						
Normalized scale score (Original model estimate)	−0.003	−0.003	−0.003	−0.004	−0.004	−0.004
Scale score (Original estimate x standard deviation)	−0.027	−0.128	−0.121	−0.141	−0.098	−0.154
Scale score for 12 months cum. deployment (Original estimate x standard deviation x 12 months)	−0.330	−1.536	−1.457	−1.691	−1.181	−1.854
Percentage difference in scale score for 12 months cumulative deployment (Original estimate x standard deviation x 12 months /(scale score Max-Min) * 100)	−0.48	−0.91	−0.95	−1.13	−0.41	−0.39

Table D.3
**The Relationship Between Deployment and Achievement Test Scores:
Cumulative Months of Deployment Modeled as Six Categorical Variables**

	Estimate (Robust Standard Error)					
	North Carolina				Washington	
	Reading	Math	English	Algebra	Reading	Math
Has deployed 1–6 months	0.001 (0.009)	−0.002 (0.008)	−0.033 (0.029)	−0.005 (0.032)	0.001 (0.024)	0.013 (0.025)
Has deployed 7–12 months	−0.018* (0.010)	−0.018* (0.009)	−0.059* (0.028)	−0.069* (0.031)	−0.010 (0.022)	−0.009 (0.023)
Has deployed 13–18 months	−0.026* (0.012)	−0.031** (0.012)	−0.042 (0.037)	−0.072 (0.041)	−0.041 (0.024)	−0.017 (0.024)
Has deployed 19–24 months	−0.059** (0.018)	−0.062** (0.017)	−0.089 (0.058)	−0.068 (0.068)	−0.135** (0.039)	−0.146** (0.039)
Has deployed 25+ months	−0.059* (0.028)	−0.114** (0.026)	−0.080 (0.093)	−0.127 (0.102)	−0.131** (0.044)	−0.144** (0.045)
Component/Rank						
Active-Duty officer	0.444** (0.024)	0.427** (0.024)	0.371** (0.049)	0.288** (0.054)	0.470** (0.033)	0.545** (0.034)
Reserve/Guard enlisted	−0.006 (0.013)	0.047** (0.013)	−0.032 (0.028)	0.006 (0.032)	−0.003 (0.020)	0.021 (0.021)
Reserve/Guard officer	0.360** (0.028)	0.439** (0.028)	0.405** (0.055)	0.241** (0.065)	0.375** (0.035)	0.474** (0.036)
Seniority						
Junior	−0.133** (0.015)	−0.119** (0.014)	−0.204** (0.041)	−0.130** (0.046)	−0.200** (0.028)	−0.252** (0.028)
Mid–grade	−0.079** (0.010)	−0.079** (0.009)	−0.151** (0.023)	−0.073** (0.026)	−0.096** (0.018)	−0.085** (0.019)
Years of service	0.001 (0.001)	0.002 (0.001)	−0.004 (0.003)	0.004 (0.003)	−0.001 (0.002)	−0.002 (0.002)
N	49,554	49,982	6,847	4,762	12,902	12,960

NOTES: Also controlled for soldier race, education, age and gender, child age, gender and grade, socioeconomic status and year and cluster-adjusted for school (WA) and child (NC).

** statistically significant at 1 percent level.

* statistically significant at 5 percent level.

Junior = E1–E4/O1–O3; Mid-grade = E5–E6/O4; Senior = E7–E9/O5–O10.

Table D.4
The Relationship Between Deployment and Achievement Test Scores: Cumulative Months of Deployment

	Estimate (Robust Standard Error)					
	North Carolina				Washington	
	Reading	Math	English	Algebra	Reading	Math
Deployed 1–18 months	−0.009	−0.010	−0.046*	−0.038	−0.016	−0.004
	(0.008)	(0.007)	(0.022)	(0.023)	(0.017)	(0.018)
Deployed 19+ months	−0.047**	−0.058**	−0.085	−0.068	−0.130**	−0.142**
	(0.017)	(0.015)	(0.052)	(0.056)	(0.031)	(0.032)
Component/rank						
Active-Duty officer	0.444**	0.427**	0.370**	0.266**	0.471**	0.546**
	(0.024)	(0.024)	(0.049)	(0.052)	(0.033)	(0.034)
Reserve/Guard enlisted	−0.006	0.048**	−0.033	−0.002	−0.004	0.020
	(0.013)	(0.013)	(0.028)	(0.031)	(0.020)	(0.021)
Reserve/Guard officer	0.361**	0.439**	0.404**	0.223**	0.374**	0.473**
	(0.028)	(0.028)	(0.055)	(0.062)	(0.035)	(0.036)
Seniority						
Junior	−0.133**	−0.119**	−0.204**	−0.116**	−0.200**	−0.252**
	(0.015)	(0.014)	(0.041)	(0.044)	(0.028)	(0.028)
Mid-grade	−0.079**	−0.079**	−0.151**	−0.065**	−0.097**	−0.086**
	(0.010)	(0.009)	(0.023)	(0.025)	(0.018)	(0.019)
Years of service	0.001	0.002	−0.004	0.004	−0.001	−0.002
	(0.001)	(0.001)	(0.003)	(0.003)	(0.002)	(0.002)
N	49,554	49,982	6,847	5,141	12,902	12,960

NOTES: Also controlled for soldier race, education, age and gender, child age, gender and grade, socioeconomic status and year and cluster-adjusted for school (WA) and child (NC).

** statistically significant at 1 percent level.

* statistically significant at 5 percent level.

Junior = E1–E4/O1–O3; Mid-grade = E5–E6/O4; Senior = E7–E9/O5–O10.

Table D.5
The Relationship Between Deployment and Achievement Test Scores: Cumulative Months of Deployment and Times Deployed

	Estimate (Robust Standard Error)					
	North Carolina				Washington	
	Reading	Math	English	Algebra	Reading	Math
Deployed 1–18 months	−0.011	−0.005	−0.099**	−0.018	−0.035	−0.013
	(0.011)	(0.010)	(0.033)	(0.035)	(0.025)	(0.025)
Deployed 19+ months	−0.051*	−0.048**	−0.187**	−0.030	−0.165**	−0.158**
	(0.021)	(0.019)	(0.069)	(0.075)	(0.046)	(0.047)
Component/rank						
Active-Duty officer	0.444**	0.427**	0.365**	0.267**	0.470**	0.545**
	(0.024)	(0.024)	(0.049)	(0.052)	(0.033)	(0.034)
Reserve/Guard enlisted	−0.005	0.047**	−0.028	−0.005	−0.002	0.021
	(0.013)	(0.013)	(0.028)	(0.031)	(0.020)	(0.021)
Reserve/Guard officer	0.361**	0.439**	0.408**	0.221**	0.375**	0.474**
	(0.028)	(0.028)	(0.055)	(0.062)	(0.035)	(0.036)
Seniority						
Junior	−0.133**	−0.119**	−0.201**	−0.117**	−0.198**	−0.251**
	(0.015)	(0.014)	(0.041)	(0.044)	(0.028)	(0.029)
Mid-grade	−0.079**	−0.079**	−0.148**	−0.066**	−0.096**	−0.086**
	(0.010)	(0.009)	(0.023)	(0.025)	(0.018)	(0.019)
Years of service	0.001	0.002	−0.004	0.004	−0.001	−0.002
	(0.001)	(0.001)	(0.003)	(0.003)	(0.002)	(0.002)
Times deployed	0.002	−0.005	0.040*	−0.015	0.015	0.007
	(0.006)	(0.006)	(0.018)	(0.019)	(0.014)	(0.015)
N	49,554	49,982	6,847	5,141	12,902	12,960

NOTES: Also controlled for soldier race, education, age and gender, child age, gender and grade, socioeconomic status and year and cluster-adjusted for school (WA) and child (NC).

** statistically significant at 1 percent level.

* statistically significant at 5 percent level.

Junior = E1–E4/O1–O3; Mid-grade = E5–E6/O4; Senior = E7–E9/O5–O10.

Table D.6
The Relationship Between Deployment and Achievement Test Scores: Cumulative Months of Deployment and Grade

	Estimate (Robust Standard Error)			
	North Carolina		Washington	
	Reading[a]	Math[a]	Reading	Math
Elementary				
Has deployed 1–18 months	−0.006	−0.015	−0.009	−0.010
	(0.012)	(0.011)	(0.025)	(0.027)
Has deployed 19+ months	−0.040	−0.047	−0.139**	−0.122**
	(0.027)	(0.025)	(0.044)	(0.048)
N	24,888	31,578	5,176	5,176
Middle				
Has deployed 1–18 months	−0.010	−0.012	−0.006	−0.002
	(0.011)	(0.011)	(0.025)	(0.032)
Has deployed 19+ months	−0.069**	−0.070**	−0.161**	−0.216**
	(0.024)	(0.022)	(0.047)	(0.059)
N	24,666	24,856	4,680	4,688
High School				
Has deployed 1–18 months	−0.046*	−0.067*	−0.060	−0.004
	(0.022)	(0.029)	(0.042)	(0.033)
Has deployed 19+ months	−0.085	−0.093	−0.067	−0.070
	(0.052)	(0.066)	(0.081)	(0.063)
N	6,847	3,542	3,046	3,096

NOTES: Also controlled for soldier race, education, age and gender, child age and gender, socioeconomic status and year and cluster-adjusted for school (WA) and child (NC).

** statistically significant at 1 percent level.

* statistically significant at 5 percent level.

[a] Results for high school in North Carolina are from English I and Algebra I standardized tests.

Table D.7
The Relationship Between Deployment and Achievement Test Scores:
Cumulative Months of Deployment and Interactions of Rank and
Component

	Estimate (Robust Standard Error)					
	North Carolina				Washington	
	Reading	Math	English	Algebra	Reading	Math
Deployed 1–18 months	−0.003	−0.004	−0.019	−0.058*	0.017	0.026
	(0.010)	(0.009)	(0.028)	(0.029)	(0.023)	(0.024)
Deployed 19+ months	−0.042*	−0.054**	−0.108	−0.096	−0.084*	−0.095**
	(0.018)	(0.017)	(0.056)	(0.062)	(0.035)	(0.036)
Component/rank						
Active-Duty officer	0.477**	0.417**	0.402**	0.258**	0.520**	0.609**
	(0.032)	(0.031)	(0.070)	(0.076)	(0.050)	(0.051)
Reserve/Guard enlisted	−0.002	0.054**	−0.012	−0.025	0.044	0.060*
	(0.014)	(0.014)	(0.033)	(0.036)	(0.026)	(0.027)
Reserve/Guard officer	0.372**	0.452**	0.437**	0.175*	0.369**	0.484**
	(0.031)	(0.031)	(0.065)	(0.075)	(0.042)	(0.044)
Seniority						
Junior	−0.133**	−0.121**	−0.205**	−0.118**	−0.195**	−0.245**
	(0.015)	(0.014)	(0.041)	(0.044)	(0.028)	(0.029)
Mid-grade	−0.079**	−0.079**	−0.150**	−0.066**	−0.095**	−0.084**
	(0.010)	(0.009)	(0.023)	(0.025)	(0.018)	(0.019)
Years of service	0.001	0.001	−0.004	0.004	−0.001	−0.002
	(0.001)	(0.001)	(0.003)	(0.003)	(0.002)	(0.002)
Interaction terms						
Active-Duty officer x Deployed 1–18	−0.049	0.019	−0.067	0.009	−0.073	−0.085
	(0.033)	(0.030)	(0.089)	(0.094)	(0.060)	(0.062)
Reserve/Guard enlisted x Deployed 1–18	−0.008	−0.015	−0.065	0.052	−0.088**	−0.069
	(0.015)	(0.014)	(0.045)	(0.047)	(0.035)	(0.036)
Reserve Guard officer x Deployed 1–18	−0.029	−0.037	−0.106	0.090	0.049	0.007
	(0.032)	(0.030)	(0.103)	(0.114)	(0.058)	(0.060)
Active-Duty officer x Deployed 19+	−0.062	−0.024	0.041	0.060	−0.097	−0.204
	(0.062)	(0.058)	(0.185)	(0.177)	(0.112)	(0.115)
Reserve/Guard enlisted x Deployed 19+	0.020	0.000	0.348	0.018	−0.241*	−0.171
	(0.054)	(0.049)	(0.179)	(0.213)	(0.100)	(0.101)
Reserve/Guard officer x Deployed 19+	−0.021	0.082	0.100	0.889*	−0.312	−0.384
	(0.105)	(0.097)	(0.365)	(0.430)	(0.228)	(0.236)
N	49,554	49,982	6,847	5,141	12,902	12,960

NOTES: Also controlled for soldier race, education, age and gender, child age, gender and
grade, socioeconomic status and year and cluster-adjusted for school (WA) and child (NC).
** statistically significant at 1 percent level.
* statistically significant at 5 percent level.

Table D.8
**The Relationship Between Deployment and Achievement Test Scores:
Cumulative Months of Deployment and Interactions for Seniority**

	Estimate (Robust Standard Error)					
	North Carolina				Washington	
	Reading	Math	English	Algebra	Reading	Math
Deployed 1–18 months	−0.007	−0.016	−0.043	−0.044	−0.018	0.011
	(0.011)	(0.011)	(0.030)	(0.031)	(0.026)	(0.027)
Deployed 19+ months	−0.050*	−0.067**	−0.010	−0.015	−0.127**	−0.172**
	(0.022)	(0.021)	(0.068)	(0.076)	(0.049)	(0.050)
Component/rank						
Active-Duty officer	0.444**	0.425**	0.368**	0.264**	0.470**	0.545**
	(0.025)	(0.024)	(0.049)	(0.052)	(0.033)	(0.034)
Reserve/Guard enlisted	−0.006	0.049**	−0.036	−0.004	−0.005	0.020
	(0.013)	(0.013)	(0.028)	(0.031)	(0.020)	(0.021)
Reserve/Guard officer	0.360**	0.440**	0.403**	0.220**	0.373**	0.474**
	(0.028)	(0.028)	(0.055)	(0.062)	(0.035)	(0.036)
Seniority						
Junior	−0.126**	−0.127**	−0.185**	−0.105	−0.214**	−0.259**
	(0.017)	(0.016)	(0.050)	(0.054)	(0.035)	(0.036)
Mid-grade	−0.080**	−0.083**	−0.145**	−0.070*	−0.092**	−0.072**
	(0.012)	(0.011)	(0.031)	(0.032)	(0.026)	(0.027)
Years of service	0.001	0.002	−0.004	0.003	−0.001	−0.002
	(0.001)	(0.001)	(0.003)	(0.003)	(0.002)	(0.002)
Interaction terms						
Junior x Deployed 1–18	−0.021	0.017	−0.051	−0.032	0.033	0.013
	(0.020)	(0.019)	(0.070)	(0.073)	(0.045)	(0.046)
Mid-grade x Deployed 1–18	0.001	0.007	0.004	0.022	−0.008	−0.039
	(0.014)	(0.013)	(0.042)	(0.043)	(0.034)	(0.035)
Junior x Deployed 19+	0.047	0.046	0.072	0.083	−0.017	0.016
	(0.062)	(0.058)	(0.226)	(0.225)	(0.109)	(0.112)
Mid-grade x Deployed 19+	0.004	0.012	−0.182	−0.132	−0.008	0.044
	(0.029)	(0.027)	(0.098)	(0.108)	(0.060)	(0.062)
N	49,554	49,982	6,847	5,141	12,902	12,960

NOTES: Also controlled for soldier race, education, age and gender, child age, gender and
grade, socioeconomic status and year and cluster-adjusted for school (WA) and child (NC).

** statistically significant at 1 percent level.

* statistically significant at 5 percent level.

Table D.9
The Relationship Between Deployment and Achievement Test Scores: Cumulative Months of Deployment and Interactions for Soldier-Parent Gender

	Estimate (Robust Standard Error)					
	North Carolina				Washington	
	Reading	Math	English	Algebra	Reading	Math
Deployed 1–18 months	−0.007 (0.008)	−0.015 (0.009)	−0.037 (0.023)	−0.035 (0.025)	−0.022 (0.018)	−0.016 (0.018)
Deployed 19+ months	−0.040* (0.017)	−0.120** (0.020)	−0.087 (0.053)	−0.072 (0.057)	−0.128** (0.032)	−0.147** (0.033)
Component/rank						
Active-Duty officer	0.444** (0.024)	0.341** (0.020)	0.369** (0.049)	0.266** (0.052)	0.471** (0.033)	0.546** (0.034)
Reserve/Guard enlisted	−0.006 (0.013)	0.039** (0.011)	−0.034 (0.028)	−0.003 (0.031)	−0.003 (0.020)	0.021 (0.021)
Reserve/Guard officer	0.361** (0.028)	0.395** (0.022)	0.403** (0.055)	0.222** (0.062)	0.375** (0.035)	0.475** (0.036)
Seniority						
Junior	−0.134** (0.015)	−0.192** (0.015)	−0.205** (0.041)	−0.116** (0.044)	−0.201** (0.028)	−0.252** (0.028)
Mid-grade	−0.079** (0.010)	−0.107** (0.009)	−0.150** (0.023)	−0.065** (0.025)	−0.097** (0.018)	−0.087** (0.019)
Years of service	0.001 (0.001)	0.000 (0.001)	−0.004** (0.003)	0.004 (0.003)	−0.001 (0.002)	−0.002 (0.002)
Female soldier	−0.004 (0.020)	0.000 (0.017)	−0.006 (0.041)	0.053 (0.043)	0.005 (0.033)	0.010 (0.034)
Interaction terms						
Female soldier x Deployed 1–18	−0.020 (0.025)	0.006 (0.027	−0.095 (0.070)	−0.031 (0.070)	0.071 (0.056)	0.144** (0.058)
Female soldier x Deployed 19+	−0.160* (0.078)	0.018 (0.099)	0.131 (0.247)	0.105 (0.251)	−0.112 (0.139)	−0.008 (0.142)
N	49,554	49,982	6,847	5,141	12,902	12,960

NOTES: Also controlled for soldier race, education, and age, child age, gender, and grade, socioeconomic status and year and cluster-adjusted for school (WA) and child (NC).

** statistically significant at 1 percent level.

* statistically significant at 5 percent level.

Table D.10
The Relationship Between Deployment and Achievement Test Scores: Cumulative Months of Deployment and Interactions for Child Gender

	Estimate (Robust Standard Error)					
	North Carolina				Washington	
	Reading	Math	English	Algebra	Reading	Math
Deployed 1–18 months	0.000 (0.010)	−0.009 (0.010)	−0.056 (0.030)	−0.035 (0.031)	−0.018 (0.023)	−0.017 (0.024)
Deployed 19+ months	−0.063** (0.022)	−0.058** (0.021)	−0.059 (0.072)	−0.066 (0.073)	−0.118** (0.043)	−0.167** (0.044)
Component/rank						
Active-Duty officer	0.445** (0.024)	0.427** (0.024)	0.371** (0.049)	0.266** (0.052)	0.471** (0.033)	0.546** (0.034)
Reserve/Guard enlisted	−0.006 (0.013)	0.048** (0.013)	−0.033 (0.028)	−0.002 (0.031)	−0.004 (0.020)	0.020 (0.021)
Reserve/Guard officer	0.361** (0.028)	0.439** (0.028)	0.404** (0.055)	0.222** (0.062)	0.374** (0.035)	0.473** (0.036)
Seniority						
Junior	−0.133** (0.015)	−0.119** (0.014)	−0.204** (0.041)	−0.116** (0.044)	−0.200** (0.028)	−0.251** (0.028)
Mid-grade	−0.079** (0.010)	−0.079** (0.009)	−0.151** (0.023)	−0.065** (0.025)	−0.097** (0.018)	−0.086** (0.019)
Years of service	0.001 (0.001)	0.002 (0.001)	−0.004 (0.003)	0.004 (0.003)	−0.001 (0.002)	−0.002 (0.002)
Male child	−0.184** (0.013)	−0.019 (0.013)	−0.246** (0.027)	0.015 (0.028)	−0.243** (0.022)	−0.051* (0.023)
Interaction terms						
Male child x Deployed 1–18	−0.017 (0.013)	−0.003 (0.012)	0.020 (0.039)	−0.005 (0.041)	0.004 (0.030)	0.026 (0.031)
Male child x Deployed 19+	0.034 (0.029)	0.000 (0.027)	−0.050 (0.095)	−0.004 (0.104)	−0.022 (0.056)	0.048 (0.058)
N	49,554	49,982	6,847	5,141	12,902	12,960

NOTES: Also controlled for soldier race, education, age and gender, child age, grade, socioeconomic status and year and cluster-adjusted for school (WA) and child (NC).

** statistically significant at 1 percent level.

* statistically significant at 5 percent level.

Table D.11
The Relationship Between Deployment and Achievement Test Scores: Cumulative Months of Deployment and Interactions for Year

	Estimate (Robust Standard Error)					
	North Carolina				Washington	
	Reading	Math	English	Algebra	Reading	Math
Deployed 1–18 months	−0.015 (0.009)	−0.016* (0.008)	−0.092** (0.032)	−0.063 (0.036)	0.023 (0.024)	−0.038 (0.025)
Deployed 19+ months	−0.102 (0.072)	−0.014 (0.065)	0.018 (0.282)	−0.531 (0.422)	0.034 (0.144)	−0.200 (0.148)
Component/rank						
Active-Duty officer	0.446** (0.013)	0.429** (0.024)	0.379** (0.049)	0.286** (0.054)	0.474** (0.033)	0.544** (0.034)
Reserve/Guard enlisted	−0.008 (0.013)	0.046** (0.013)	−0.046 (0.028)	−0.000 (0.032)	−0.002 (0.020)	0.018 (0.021)
Reserve/Guard officer	0.359** (0.028)	0.438** (0.028)	0.398** (0.055)	0.234** (0.065)	0.375** (0.035)	0.470** (0.036)
Seniority						
Junior	−0.133** (0.015)	−0.118** (0.014)	−0.211** (0.040)	−0.130** (0.046)	−0.206** (0.028)	−0.248** (0.029)
Mid-grade	−0.079** (0.010)	−0.079** (0.009)	−0.156** (0.023)	−0.074** (0.026)	−0.099** (0.018)	−0.085** (0.019)
Years of service	0.001 (0.001)	0.002 (0.001)	−0.005 (0.003)	0.003 (0.003)	−0.001 (0.002)	−0.002 (0.002)
Interaction terms						
2005 x Deployed 1–18	0.001 (0.014)	0.002 (0.013)	−0.068 (0.057)	−0.009 (0.061)	—	—
2006 x Deployed 1–18	0.006 (0.016)	0.010 (0.015)	0.068 (0.061)	0.052 (0.069)	−0.048 (0.043)	0.061 (0.045)
2007 x Deployed 1–18	0.003 (0.017)	−0.012 (0.015)	0.136** (0.064)	0.012 (0.068)	−0.092* (0.046)	−0.019 (0.047)
2008 x Deployed 1–18	—	—	—	—	−0.020 (0.046)	0.090 (0.048)
2005 x Deployed 19+	0.066 (0.039)	0.002 (0.070)	−0.150 (0.331)	0.494 (0.455)	—	—
2006 x Deployed 19+	0.058 (0.075)	0.032 (0.067)	−0.124 (0.297)	0.561 (0.435)	−0.134 (0.162)	0.187 (0.167)
2007 x Deployed 19+	0.058 (0.074)	0.069 (0.067)	−0.036 (0.292)	0.401 (0.430)	−0.172 (0.154)	0.033 (0.159)
2008 x Deployed 19+	—	—	—	—	−0.190 (0.152)	0.051 (0.156)
N	49,554	49,982	6,847	4,762	12,902	12,960

NOTES: Also controlled for soldier race, education, age and gender, child age, grade, socioeconomic status and year and cluster-adjusted for school (WA) and child (NC).

** statistically significant at 1 percent level.

* statistically significant at 5 percent level.

Bibliography

Andrews, K., K. Bencio, J. Brown, L. Conwell, C. Fahlman, and E. Schone, *Health Care Survey of DOD Beneficiaries 2008 Annual Report*, Washington, D.C.: Mathematica Policy Research, Inc., 2008.

Angrist, J.D., and J.H. Johnson, IV, "Effects of Work-Related Absences on Families: Evidence from the Gulf War," *Industrial and Labor Relations Review*, Vol. 54, No. 1, October 2000, pp. 41–58.

Armbruster, P., and J. Lichtman, "Are School Based Mental Health Services Effective? Evidence from 36 Inner City Schools," *Community Mental Health Journal*, Vol. 35, No. 6, 1999, pp. 493–504.

Bonds, Timothy M., Dave Baiocchi, and Laurie L. McDonald, *Army Deployments to OIF and OEF*, Santa Monica, Calif.: RAND Corporation, DB-587-A, 2010. http://www.rand.org/pubs/documented_briefings/DB587.html

Branz-Spall, Angela Maria, and Roger Rosenthal, with Al Wright, "Children of the Road: Migrant Students, Our Nation's Most Mobile Population," *Journal of Negro Education*, Vol. 72, No. 1, Winter 2003.

Castaneda, Laura Werber, Margaret C. Harrell, Danielle M. Varda, Kimberly Curry Hall, Megan K. Beckett, and Stefanie Stern, *Deployment Experiences of Guard and Reserve Families: Implications for Support and Retention*, Santa Monica, Calif.: RAND Corporation, MG-645-OSD, 2008. http://www.rand.org/pubs/monographs/MG645.html

Chandra, Anita, Rachel M. Burns, Terri L. Tanielian, Lisa Jaycox, and Molly M. Scott, *Understanding the Impact of Deployment on Children and Families: Findings from a Pilot Study of Operation Purple Camp Participants*, Santa Monica, Calif.: RAND Corporation, WR-566, 2008. http://www.rand.org/pubs/working_papers/WR566.html

Chandra, Anita, Sandraluz Lara-Cinisomo, Lisa Jaycox, Terri Tanielian, Rachel Burns, Teague Ruder, and Bing Han, "Children on the Homefront: The Experience of Children from Military Families," *Pediatrics*, Vol. 125, No. 1, January 2010, pp. 13–22.

Chandra, Anita, Sandraluz Lara-Cinisomo, Lisa H. Jaycox, Terri Tanielian, Bing Han, Rachel M. Burns, and Teague Ruder, *Views from the Homefront: The Experiences of Youth and Spouses from Military Families*, Santa Monica, Calif.: RAND Corporation, TR-913-NMFA. 2011.
http://www.rand.org/pubs/technical_reports/TR913.html

Chartrand, M., D.A. Frank, L.F. White, and T.R. Shope, "Effect of Parents' Wartime Deployment on Behavior of Young Children in Military Families," *Archives of Pediatric & Adolescent Medicine*, Vol. 162, No. 11, 2008, pp. 1009–1014.

Chisolm, D.J., W. Gardner, T. Julian, and K.J. Kelleher, "Adolescent Satisfaction with Computer-Assisted Behavioral Risk Screening in Primary Care," *Child and Adolescent Mental Health*, 2007.

Clarke, G., W. Hawkins, M. Murphy, et al., "Targeted Prevention of Unipolar Depressive Disorder in an At-Risk Sample of High School Adolescents: A Randomized Trial of a Group Cognitive Intervention," *Journal of the American Academy of Child and Adolescent Psychiatry*, Vol. 34, 1995, pp. 312–321.

Cohen, Sharon, "The Long Haul: Heroism Under Fire," *Memphis Commercial Appeal*, August 8, 2008.

Coltrane, S., "Research on Household Labor: Modeling and Measuring the Social Embeddedness of Routine Family Work," *Journal of Marriage and Family*, Vol. 62, No. 4, 2000, pp. 1208–1233.

Conger, D., and M. Finkelstein, "Foster Care and School Mobility," *Journal of Negro Education*, Vol. 72, No. 1, 2003, pp. 97–103.

Cox, Matthew, "Tempo to Increase in Short Term, Casey Says," *ArmyTimes.com*, May 13, 2009.

Defense Manpower Data Center (DMDC), *Profile of Service Members Ever Deployed*, June 29, 2009.

Defense Manpower Data Center (DMDC), Survey and Program Evaluation Division, *2006 Survey of Active Duty Spouses: Tabulations of Responses*, Arlington, Va.: Defense Manpower Data Center Survey & Program Evaluation Division, DMDC Report No. 2006-033, January 2007.

Department of Defense, *Demographics 2007: Profile of the Military Community*, Washington, D.C.: Department of Defense, 2007.

Department of Defense and Department of Education, "Memorandum of Understanding between the Department of Defense and the Department of Education," signed June 25, 2008. As of June 16, 2010:
http://www.defense.gov/news/d20080625doddoe1.pdf

Department of Defense Task Force on Mental Health, *An Achievable Vision: Report of the Department of Defense Task Force on Mental Health*, Falls Church, Va.: Defense Health Board, 2007.

Duplechain, Rosalind, Ronald Reigner, and Abbot Packard, "Striking Differences: The Impact of Moderate and High Trauma on Reading Achievement," *Reading Psychology,* Vol. 29, No. 2, March 2008, pp. 117–136.

Engel, R.C., L.B. Gallagher, and D.S. Lyle, "Military Deployments and Children's Academic Achievement: Evidence from Department of Defense Education Activity Schools," *Economics of Education Review,* Vol. 29, Issue. 1, 2010, pp. 73–82.

Ensminger, M., and A. Slusarcick, "Paths to High School Graduation or Dropout: A Longitudinal Study of a First-Grade Cohort," *Sociology of Education,* Vol. 65, April 1992, pp. 95–112.

Faran, Michael E., "Systems of Mental Health Care: The Role of 'Communities of Practice,'" unpublished. As of June 16, 2010:
http://www.health.mil/content/docs/dcoe/Day_2.13_Systems_of_Care.Faran.pdf

Flake, Eric, Beth Ellen Davis, Patti L. Johnson, and Laura S. Middleton, "The Psychosocial Effects of Deployment on Military Children," *Journal of Developmental & Behavioral Pediatrics,* Vol. 30, 2009, pp. 271–278.

Fong, Lillian G., and Jewelle Taylor Gibbs, "Facilitating Services to Multicultural Communities in a Dominant Culture Setting: An Organizational Perspective," *Administration in Social Work,* Vol. 19, No. 2, 1995, pp. 1–24.

Freedberg, Sydney J., "The Army's Growing Pains: Troop Strength Is Rising, But Can the Army Grow Faster Than Iraq and Afghanistan Are Wearing It Out?" *National Journal Magazine,* September 19, 2009.

"Ft. Bragg, N.C.," *The Military Zone.* As of August 10, 2009:
http://themilitaryzone.com/bases/fort_bragg.html

García-Lizana, Francisca, and Ingrid Muñoz-Mayorga, "What About Telepsychiatry? A Systematic Review," *Primary Care Companion to The Journal of Clinical Psychiatry,* Vol. 12, No. 2, 2010.

Gibbs, Deborah A., Sandra L. Martin, Lawrence L. Kupper, and Ruby E. Johnson, "Child Maltreatment in Enlisted Soldiers' Families During Combat-Related Deployments," *JAMA: Journal of the American Medical Association,* Vol. 298, No. 5, August 2007.

Gillham, J., K. Reivich, L. Jaycox, et al., "Prevention of Depressive Symptoms in School Children: Two-Year Follow-Up," *Psychological Science,* Vol. 6, 1995, pp. 343–351.

Ginsburg, Paul B., Myles Maxfield, Ann S. O'Malley, Deborah Peikes, Hoangmai H. Pham, "Making Medical Homes Work: Moving from Concept to Practice." Washington, D.C.: Center for Studying Health System Change, Policy Perspective No. 1, December 2008. As of February 2011:
http:/www.hschange.com/CONTENT/1030/?words+au=16

Glied, S., and A.E. Cuellar, "Trends and Issues in Child and Adolescent Mental Health," *Health Affairs,* Vol. 22, No. 5, 2003, pp. 39–50.

Glod, M., "Coping with Their Parents' War," *Washington Post*, July 17, 2008.

Gorman, G.H., M. Eide, and E. Hisle-Gorman, "Wartime Military Deployment and Increased Pediatric Mental and Behavioral Health Complaints," *Pediatrics*, November 8, 2010.

Hill, Carolyn J., Howard S. Bloom, Alison Rebeck Black, and Mark W. Lipsey, "Empirical Benchmarks for Interpreting Effect Sizes in Research," *Child Development Perspectives*, Vol. 2, No. 3, December 2008, pp. 172–177.

Hoge, C.W., C.A. Castro, S.C. Messer, D. McGurk, D.I. Cotting, and R.L. Koffman, "Combat Duty in Iraq and Afghanistan, Mental Health Problems, and Barriers to Care," *New England Journal of Medicine,* Vol. 351, No. 1, 2004, pp. 13–22.

Hoover, Stephan S., M. Weist, S. Kataoka, S. Adelsheim, and C. Mills, "Transformation of Children's Mental Health Services: The Role of School Mental Health," *Psychiatric Services*, Vol. 58, 2007, pp. 1330–1338.

Horwitz, S.M., P.J. Leaf, J.M. Leventhal, B. Forsyth, and K.N. Speechley, "Identification and Management of Psychosocial and Developmental Problems in Community-Based, Primary Care Pediatric Practices," *Pediatrics,* Vol. 89, 1992, pp. 480–485.

Hosek, Jim, and Francisco Martorell, *How Have Deployments During the War on Terrorism Affected Reenlistment?* Santa Monica, Calif.: RAND Corporation, MG-873-OSD, 2009.

Huebner, A., and J. Mancini, *Adjustments Among Adolescents in Military Families When a Parent Is Deployed,* Purdue University, 2005.

Installation Guide: Ft. Bragg, N.C., Military.com. As of August 10, 2009: http://benefits.military.com/misc/installations/Base_Content.jsp?id=3760

Installation Guide: Ft. Lewis, Military.com. As of August 10, 2009: http://img.military.com/misc/installations/Base_Content.jsp?id=5050

Institute of Medicine (IOM), *Returning Home from Iraq and Afghanistan: Preliminary Assessment of Readjustment Needs of Veterans, Servicemembers, and Their Families,* Washington, D.C.: The National Academies Press, 2010.

Jensen, P.S., D. Grogan, S.N. Xenakis, and M.W. Bain, "Father Absence: Effects on Child and Maternal Psychopathology," *Journal of the American Academy of Child and Adolescent Psychiatry*, Vol. 28, No. 5, 1989, p. 805.

Jensen, Peter, David Martin, and Henry Watanabe, "Children's Response to Parental Separation During Operation Desert Storm," *Journal of the American Academy of Child and Adolescent Psychiatry*, Vol. 35, No. 4, April 1996.

Juvonen, Jaana, Adrienne Nishina, and Sandra Graham, "Peer Harassment, Psychological Adjustment, and School Functioning in Early Adolescence," *Journal of Educational Psychology*, Vol. 92, 2000, pp. 349–359.

Karney, Benjamin R., and John S. Crown, *Families Under Stress: An Assessment of Data, Theory, and Research on Marriage and Divorce in the Military*, Santa Monica, Calif.: RAND Corporation, MG-599-OSD, 2007.
http://www.rand.org/pubs/monographs/MG599.html

Kataoka, S., L. Zhang, and K. Wells, "Unmet Need for Mental Health Care Among U.S. Children: Variation by Ethnicity and Insurance Status," *American Journal of Psychiatry*, Vol. 159, No. 9, 2002, pp. 1548–1555.

Kelleher, K.J., G.E. Childs, R.C. Wasserman, T.K. McInerny, P.A. Nutting, and W.P. Gardner, "Insurance Status and Recognition of Psychosocial Problems: A Report from the Pediatric Research in Office Settings and the Ambulatory Sentinel Practice Networks," *Archives of Pediatrics and Adolescent Medicine,* Vol. 151, 1997, pp. 1109–1114.

Kim, Wun Jung, "Child and Adolescent Psychiatry Workforce: A Critical Shortage and National Challenge," *Academic Psychiatry*, Vol. 27, December 2003, pp. 277–282.

Koppelman, J., *The Provider System for Children's Mental Health: Workforce Capacity and Effective Treatment,* NHPF Issue Brief No. 801, October 26, 2004.

Leventhal, T., J. Graber, and J. Brooks-Gunn, "Adolescent Transitions to Young Adulthood: Antecedents, Correlates and Consequences of Adolescent Employment," *Journal of Research on Adolescence*, Vol. 11, 2001, pp. 297–323.

Lyle, David S., "Using Military Deployments and Job Assignments to Estimate the Effect of Parental Absences and Household Relocations on Children's Academic Achievement," *Journal of Labor Economics,* Vol. 24, No. 2, 2006.

Margolin, Gayla, and Elana B. Gordis, "The Effects of Family and Community Violence on Children," *Annual Review of Psychology*, Vol. 51, 2000, pp. 445–479.

McKay, Mary M., Richard Hibbert, Kimberly Hoagwood, James Rodriguez, Laura Murray, Joanna Legerski, and David Fernandez, "Integrating Evidence-Based Engagement Interventions into 'Real World' Child Mental Health Settings," *Brief Treatment and Crisis Intervention,* Vol. 4, No. 2, Oxford University Press, 2004.

Mental Health Advisory Team (MHAT-III), Operation Iraqi Freedom 04-06, *Report,* Office of the Surgeon, Multinational Force–Iraq and Office of the Surgeon General, U.S. Army Medical Command, May 29, 2006a. As of January 24, 2011:
http://www.armymedicine.army.mil/reports/mhat/mhat_iii/mhat-iii.cfm

Mental Health Advisory Team (MHAT-IV), Operation Iraqi Freedom 05-07, *Final Report,* Office of the Surgeon, Multinational Force–Iraq and Office of the Surgeon General, U.S. Army Medical Command, November 17, 2006b. As of February 2011:
http://www.armymedicine.army.mil/reports/mhat/mhat_iv/MHAT_IV_Report_17NOV06.pdf

Morse, J., *The New Emotional Cycles of Deployment,* PDF file retrieved June 28, 2007, from the U.S. Department of Defense: Deployment Health and Family Readiness Library: San Diego, Calif. As of September 1, 2010: http://www.hooah4health.com/deployment/familymatters/emotionalcycle.htm/

Moyers, Theresa B., and Stephen Rollnick, "A Motivational Interviewing Perspective on Resistance in Psychotherapy," *Journal of Clinical Psychology,* Vol. 58, Issue 2, 2006, pp. 185–193.

Myers, Kathleen M., Jeanette M. Valentine, and Sanford M. Melzer, "Child and Adolescent Telepsychiatry: Utilization and Satisfaction," *Telemedicine and e-Health,* Vol. 14, No. 2, March 2008, pp. 131–137.

National Center for Interstate Compacts, "Interstate Compact on Educational Opportunity for Military Children State-by-State Legislative Status, Updated June 9, 2010." As of June 16, 2010: http://www.csg.org/programs/policyprograms/NCIC/documents/DODState-by-statechart6-9-10_000.pdf

National Institute for Health Care Management, "Strategies to Support the Integration of Mental Health into Pediatric Primary Care," Issue Paper, August 2009. As of June 16, 2010: http://nihcm.org/pdf/PediatricMH-FINAL.pdf

Nelson, Eve-Lynn, Martha Barnard, and Sharon Cain, "Treating Childhood Depression over Videoconferencing," *Telemedicine Journal and e-Health,* Vol. 9, No. 1, March 2003, pp. 49–55.

New Freedom Commission on Mental Health, *Achieving the Promise: Transforming Mental Health Care in America,* Final Report, 2003. As of February 2011: http://web.archive.org/web/20041020125641/www.openminds.com/indres/finalnewfreedom.pdf

"North Carolina End-of-Course Tests," As of November 23, 2010: http://www.ncpublicschools.org/accountability/testing/eoc/

Operation Iraqi Freedom (OIF) Mental Health Advisory Team (MHAT), *Report,* U.S. Army Surgeon General and HQDA G-1, December 16, 2003. As of January 24, 2011: http://www.pbs.org/wgbh/pages/frontline/shows/heart/readings/mhat.pdf

Operation Iraqi Freedom (OIF-II) Mental Health Advisory Team (MHAT-II), *Report,* U.S. Army Surgeon General, January 30, 2005. As of January 24, 2011: http://www.armymedicine.army.mil/reports/mhat/mhat_ii/OIF-II_REPORT.pdf

Pignatiello, Antonio, Katherine Boydell, John Teshima, and Tiziana Volpe, "Supporting Primary Care Through Pediatric Telepsychiatry," *Canadian Journal of Community Mental Health,* Vol. 27, No. 2, Fall 2008, pp. 139–151.

Pisano, Mark Charles, *The Children of Operation Desert Storm: An Analysis of California Achievement Test Scores in Sixth Graders of Deployed and Nondeployed Parents,* Ph.D. dissertation, Campbell University, 1992.

Richardson, L.P., C.W. Lewis, M. Casey-Goldstein, E. McCauley, and W. Katon, "Pediatric Primary Care Providers and Adolescent Depression: A Qualitative Study of Barriers to Treatment and the Effect of the Black Box Warning," *Journal of Adolescent Health,* Vol. 40, No. 5, 2007, pp. 433–439.

Rollnick, S., N. Heather, and A. Bell, "Negotiating Behavior Change in Medical Settings: The Development of Brief Motivational Interviewing," *Journal of Mental Health,* Vol. 1, 1992, pp. 25–37.

Russell, R., M. Faran, C. Ivany, V. Venezia, D. Crowley, N. Hartvigsen, and N. Ellis, "Distribution and Availability of Child and Adolescent Psychiatrists to the Youth of Active Duty Military Worldwide and a Comparison with Civilian Youth in the US," 2008, unpublished.

Saltzman, William R., Robert S. Pynoos, Alan M. Steinberg, Eugene Aisenberg, and Christopher M. Layne, "Trauma and Grief-Focused Intervention for Adolescents Exposed to Community Violence," *Group Dynamics: Theory, Research & Practice,* Vol. 5, 2001, pp. 291–303.

Schumm, W.R., D.B. Bell, B. Knott, and R.E. Rice, "The Perceived Effect of Stressors on Marital Satisfaction Among Civilian Wives of Enlisted Soldiers Deployed to Somalia for Operation Restore Hope," *Military Medicine,* Vol. 161, 1996, pp. 601–606.

Schwartz, David, and Andrea Gorman, "Community Violence Exposure and Children's Academic Functioning," *Journal of Educational Psychology,* Vol. 95, 2003, pp. 163–173.

Szapocznik, J., A. Perez-Vidal, A.L. Brickman, F.H. Foote, D.A. Santisteban, O.E. Hervis, and W.M. Kurtines. "Engaging Adolescent Drug Abusers and Their Families into Treatment: A Strategic Structural Systems Approach," *Journal of Consulting and Clinical Psychology,* Vol. 56, 1988, pp. 552–557.

Thomas, Christopher R., and Charles E. Holzer III, "National Distribution of Child and Adolescent Psychiatrists," *Journal of the American Academy of Child & Adolescent Psychiatry,* Vol. 38, No. 1, 1999, pp. 9–15.

Thomas, Christopher R., MD, and Charles E. Holzer III, Ph.D., "The Continuing Shortage of Child and Adolescent Psychiatrists," *Journal of the American Academy of Child & Adolescent Psychiatry,* Vol. 45, Issue 9, pp. 1023–1031, September 2006.

U.S. Department of Agriculture, "Adopt-A-School Program Guide: Agriculture and Education, Planting the Seeds of Opportunity," May 1999. As of June 16, 2010:
http://www.usda.gov/news/pubs/adoptsch.pdf

Whitmore Schanzenbach, Diane, "What Have Researchers Learned from Project Star?" Chicago, Ill.: Harris School Working Paper, Series 06.06, August 2006.

Wise, Lindsay, "Part-Timers Go Full Force," *Houston Chronicle*, January 31, 2010.

Wong, Leonard, and Stephen Gerras, *The Effects of Multiple Deployments on Army Adolescents,* Strategic Studies Institute, January 2010.

Word, Elizabeth, et al., *The State of Tennessee's Student/Teacher Achievement Ratio (STAR) Project: Final Summary Report,* Tennessee State Department of Education, 1990.

Yule, William, and Ann Gold, *Wise Before the Event: Coping with Crises in Schools,* London: Calouste Gulbenkian Foundation, 1993, reprinted 2006.

Zimmer, Ron, Brian Gill, Kevin Booker, Stephane Lavertu, Tim R. Sass, and John Witte, *Charter Schools in Eight States: Effects on Achievement, Attainment, Integration and Competition,* Santa Monica, Calif.: RAND Corporation, MG-869-BMG/JOY/WPF, 2009.